The Continual Improvement Process

The Continual Improvement Process

From Strategy to the Bottom Line

Craig Cochran

Paton Press LLC
Chico, California

Most Paton Press books are available at quantity discounts when purchased in bulk. For more information, contact:

Paton Press LLC
PO Box 44
Chico, CA 95927-0044
Telephone: (530) 342-5480
Fax: (530) 342-5471
E-mail: *books@patonpress.com*
Web: *www.patonpress.com*

06 05 04 03 02 01   5 4 3 2 1

ISBN 0-9713231-8-6

Staff

Publisher ....Scott M. Paton
Editors...Heidi M. Paton, Finn Kraemer, and Taran March
Book Design...Caylen Balmain

Dedicated to P.C. and Linda Cochran,
who taught me my first lessons about improvement

There is no one giant step that does it.
It's a lot of little steps.

—*Peter A. Cohen*

Contents

Acknowledgments

I'd like to offer my special thanks to the following people and organizations for their assistance in developing this book: Muriel, Brynn, and Cullen Cochran; P.C. and Linda Cochran; John and Rocio Lancaster; Dr. Brett Saks, Kim Saks, and Aaron Saks—Dynamic Chiropractic & Acupuncture Clinics, PC (Chandler, AZ); Mrs. Thelma O'Dell; Rosemarie Kobau—Centers for Disease Control and Prevention (Atlanta, GA); Lee Crayfish Coursey; Michael Stamp, Jeff Besh, and Marvin Sewell—SI Corp. (Chickamauga, GA); Debbie Ellis— See Rock City Inc. (Lookout Mountain, GA); John Thomas; Paolo Chiappina—Sara Lee Inc. (Winston-Salem, NC); Donna Ennis, Charlette Price, Vicki Bryan, Deann Desai, Dennis Kelly, Holly Lawe, Tim Israel, Phil Callner, Carol Aton, Elliot Price, Don Pital, David Apple, Jerry Zolkowski, Karen Brown, Larry Alford, Bob Springfield, Rick Duke, and the entire staff of the Economic Development Institute—Georgia Institute of Technology (Atlanta, GA); Scott Paton, Heidi Paton, Christel Whetstone, Finn Kraemer, Erin Sullivan—Paton Press (Chico, CA); Robert Green, Caylen Balmain, Dirk Dusharme, Laurel Thoennes—*Quality Digest* (Chico, CA); Tom Eck, Jennifer Edge—S.P. Newsprint (Dublin, GA); Donna K. Tierney—Naval Facilities Institute (San Diego, CA); Jim Hineline—Briggs & Stratton Power Products (Jefferson, WI); Michon Mitchell, Lynn Ann Pall, Chester J. Wojna—The Coca-Cola Co. (Atlanta, GA); J. Gustavo Eiras—Coca-Cola de Argentina S.A. (Buenos Aires, Argentina); Daryl Swanstrom—Spyraflo Inc. (Peachtree City, GA); Lee Smith, Terrall Putnam, Angela Malone—YKK USA Inc. (Macon, GA); Terry Waldrop and Bob McAlister—T&D Remarketed Services (Alpharetta, GA); Bob Richards—Beaulieu of America (Dalton, GA); Gary Frost—Missouri Enterprise, University of Missouri at Rolla; Billy Ingram, Joey Milford—Interface Flooring Inc. (La Grange, GA.); Susan VanHemert— Simple Harmony Computing Services Inc. (Kennesaw, GA); Lauren Thompson, Mark Wachtendonck, Mike Thompson—I. Technical Services (Norcross, GA); Mark Mendenhall, Ph.D.—University of Tennessee at Chattanooga; Larry Whittington—Whittington Associates (Atlanta, GA); Al Pate—AshCo-Atlanta LLC (Atlanta, GA); Shawn Mewborn—TriCenturion LLC (Columbia, SC).

Chapter One

Introduction

Continual improvement is the incremental process of becoming a smarter, stronger, and more successful organization. It doesn't result from a single initiative but rather from a wide range of tools and techniques. Participants in the process also are wide-ranging; in fact, all employees in the organization must contribute to the effort, and their involvement should be limited only by their analytical and creative powers, not by their location on the organizational chart.

The words "incremental process" are important in understanding continual improvement. "Incremental" means that the effort will involve many small steps forward and probably a few steps backward. By its nature, continual improvement implies that an organization won't experience an unbroken chain of successes from its improvement efforts. The cumulative result, however, will be increased performance and long-term success. Although it would be nice to hit home runs every trip to the plate, the philosophy of continual improvement recognizes that a lot of base hits are going to win most games in the long term.

"Process" means that the effort is ongoing. It exists as an integral part of the organization, transforming inputs (e.g., creativity, enthusiasm, energy) into outputs (e.g., customer loyalty, higher revenues, profits). The continual improvement process isn't a program or project, both of which have terminal end points. Rather, the process continues for as long as the organization exists. Just like any other process within the organization, the improvement process will itself improve over time, delivering more value to the organization and its members.

The concepts described in this book don't by any means represent all the continual improvement tools and techniques in existence. However, they do represent two important attributes:

■ *They can be implemented.* These tools are practical. They're described in great detail, with explicit instructions for how they should be applied. Nearly any organization can implement these tools using its own internal resources. As long as the organization possesses competent and energetic management and a continual improvement champion who can keep everyone focused on the process, then this book will be a road map for success.

■ *They're efficient.* Having applied them in a variety of organizations, I can say that, compared to the resources they consume, these tools deliver the biggest boost to an organization. Does the continual improvement process cost money? Of course. Do the benefits far outweigh the expenses? Absolutely. These tools and techniques will pay for themselves many times over. It's worth noting that the concepts described in this book can be applied by business, governmental, and nonprofit enterprises alike.

I briefly mentioned the role of champion above. This is someone with organizational clout and strong communication skills who will help drive the continual improvement process. The words "charismatic" and "convincing" come to mind when I think about effective champions I've known in the past. Sometimes this role is filled by the chief executive officer, managing director, quality manager, or some other "titled" individual. The title, however, is meaningless. What matters is that the person has a mastery of improvement tools and techniques and can get everyone to embrace and use them in a disciplined manner. Occasionally, the champion's role is filled by someone from outside the organization. It's an unfortunate truth that outsiders often have more credibility with some people in the organization. But regardless of where the champion originates, the role is vital to the process taking root and producing positive results. Don't neglect to assign the role of continual improvement champion.

The tools described in this book are presented in roughly the same order that they should be implemented, though the order isn't necessarily critical. In many cases, the order of implementation will be driven by the most urgent issues facing the organization. Let's take a brief look at the topic of each chapter:

- *Deciding what's important.* Here we explore how mission and strategy form the starting points for everything else that takes place within the organization. Key measures are then proposed as the primary method for translating mission and strategy into concepts that everyone can grasp. This chapter presents a model for determining and defining mission, strategy, and key measures in any organization.

- *Communicating what's important.* The most important messages an organization can communicate are the details of its key measures, what they mean, and how everyone can contribute to them. Specific steps for communicating these in stages are outlined.

- *Analysis and action.* This chapter explores the forums within which key measures and other strategic information should be reviewed. Details such as frequency of review, participants, data review techniques, generation and prioritization of improvement actions, and project tracking are addressed.

- *Process orientation.* An organization's structure in relation to natural business processes has a tremendous bearing on improvement efforts. In this chapter we'll compare the effectiveness of function departments vs. integrated processes. We'll also propose some actions that any organization can implement that will incrementally move it closer to a process orientation.

- *Effective problem solving.* Very few organizations are particularly skilled at attacking problems in a disciplined, lasting way. We'll explore some of the fundamentals of effective problem solving and propose some practical tools for facilitating the process.

- *High-impact auditing.* One of the best improvement tools an organization has is its ability to look inward and determine where improvements can be made. When this is done in a systematic and planned way, it's referred to as auditing. We'll examine the auditing process as well as the types of processes it should focus on to produce the most valuable improvement opportunities.

- *Building the culture of continual improvement.* Culture is a topic that seems fuzzy to many people. Fuzzy or not, it's a reality that must be systematically addressed if an organization plans to imbed the continual improvement process into its soul. We'll examine the five foundations of a culture of continual improvement and describe how they can be put into practice.

As always, even the best guidance is worthless if it's not put into practice. Examine each of the tools and techniques proposed from this point forward and consider how they can be applied in your own organization. Then put together a continual improvement plan and start chipping away. If you don't do it, your competitors will. You must either make continual improvement one of your organization's underlying principles or be replaced by some other organization. This book should help you make the right decision and use your resources in the best manner possible.

Chapter Two

Deciding What's Important

In This Chapter
- Key Measures
- Mission and Strategy
- Key Measures Worksheet
- Documenting Key Measures

The first step in the continual improvement process is to decide what's important for your organization's success. "Decide what's important?" you shout. "Everything's important! Revenues and profits and quality and customer satisfaction and innovation and cost control and efficiency. It's all important!"

Yes, it's all important. However, there are different degrees of importance. Everything isn't equally important. Organizations often miss this point and try to focus on everything.

To receive the full benefit of the continual improvement process, an organization must focus on key measures, which are those variables that have the biggest effect on an organization's survival and competitive position. You could call them business objectives, strategic targets, big hitters, you name it. Whatever you call them, key measures are the issues that everyone in the organization must focus on. Continual improvement is about successes of all sizes and descriptions: minor and huge, short term and long term, team-based and individual—but the one consistent thread is that the successes all eventually affect what's most important to the organization.

Key measures have some very specific characteristics, all of which you'll need to become very familiar with:

■ *They're measurable.* That means we can track their progress using data. The data might be variable (an actual number, such as 97.4 percent) or an attribute (go or no-go, such as completing a project by its target date). Either way, we can understand whether progress is being made against the measure.

■ *They're the true indicators of success or failure.* Key measures are the make-or-break objectives. Your organization must succeed at key measures to survive. If you think you've determined a key measure, ask the question, "If we consistently fail at this, will we still be in business over the long term?" If the answer is yes, then you might not have a key measure. By definition, if an organization fails at a key measure, the organization itself will fail—maybe not right away, but eventually.

■ *They're used for strategic decision making.* This isn't an exercise in sticking pretty charts all over the walls; this is about managing for continual improvement. Because key measures drive actions and decisions at the highest organizational levels, it's critical that top management believes in the concept and is committed to it. Otherwise, the process will be meaningless.

■ *They're different from one organization to the next.* All organizations have different strategic concerns, so it makes sense that key measures will also differ from organization to organization. Some measures, however, are universal for business organizations: revenue and profit, for example. Companies that have high investments in capital equipment might find that return on investment is a key measure. Companies that make and stock a tangible product might discover that inventory turnover is a key measure. Companies that are highly invested in human capital (such as software development companies) will probably determine that employee retention is a key measure.

■ *They're few enough to achieve focus.* The more key measures that personnel try to concentrate on, the less focused they'll be. Start with a short list that people can understand. Most organizations will have between four and eight true key measures. Most other measures are actually intermediate measures. Keep the list of key measures tight and focused.

■ *They're representative of a wide range of concerns.* In their excellent book, *The Balanced Scorecard*, Robert Kaplan and David Norton describe using a balanced portfolio of metrics to manage by. Companies are accustomed to assessing themselves in terms of accounting measures. There are good, common-sense reasons for doing this. However, traditional accounting measures are always "backward looking"—what happened last month, last quarter, last year. Past performance isn't a guarantee of future performance, and it's entirely possible to drive yourself out of business by focusing solely on traditional accounting measures. An organization should develop a wide-ranging portfolio of measures that represent success in the short, medium, and long term. Human-resource measures such as employee turnover or hours of training per employee are perfect examples of long-term measures; they might not pay off this month—or even this year—but they provide the building blocks for success over the long term.

MISSION AND STRATEGY

Mission and strategy are the logical starting points for determining key measures. From a theoretical standpoint, it's as simple as one-two-three: mission leads to strategy, and strategy leads to key measures. Let's examine mission and strategy and see how they play out in developing key measures.

An organization's mission defines its reason for existence. The mission can't be in the form of platitudes and meaningless generalities; it must be a serious, forward-looking vision of where the organization exists within the context of its competitive environment, and where its management hopes to take it in the future. A well-written mission statement will answer many of the following questions:

■ Why do we exist?
■ Whom do we serve?
■ What needs/desires do we satisfy?
■ What goods and/or services do we provide?
■ Who are our interested parties?
■ What beliefs and values do we hold true?
■ Where are we moving as an organization?

Some organizations subdivide the topics shown above into various policy-level documents. Multiple documents such as a values statement, vision statement, or statement of purpose clutter the walls. There's nothing wrong with this approach, but remember that in most endeavors simplicity is the key to success. The more policy-level documents an organization has, the less likely people are to understand what they all mean. A streamlined, all-inclusive mission statement is the best means of getting all personnel focused together.

An organization's members must understand their mission with unambiguous certainty. It provides a rallying point and a source of pride. The mission statement also communicates the organization's purpose and why it matters to the outside world. Anybody reading a well-written mission statement will come away with an appreciation of the organization's overall intentions, values, and objectives.

Consider the fictional company Yellowjacket Technologies. The company designs, manufactures, and sells complex electronic systems for industrial and defense applications. This is their mission statement:

YELLOWJACKET TECHNOLOGIES MISSION STATEMENT

Yellowjacket Technologies strives to be the market leader in innovative electronic systems and application. We intend to push the limits of technology to provide our industrial and defense customers with cutting-edge electronic solutions for their needs. In the pursuit of these objectives, Yellowjacket embraces the following principles:

■ *Focus on the customer*

■ *Continual product innovation aimed at meeting market requirements*

■ *A creative environment that allows our people to excel*

■ *The use of metrics and goals that drive continual improvement of our overall performance*

■ *Acknowledgement of our place in the larger community and our responsibilities to our neighbors, the environment, and the public*

—Peter C. Buzz, President & CEO

The Yellowjacket Technologies mission statement paints a clear picture of the organization. The language is simple and understandable—no flowery platitudes here. It's easy to pick out the general themes:

■ Technological innovation

■ Customer focus

■ A culture that facilitates creativity

■ The use of strategic objectives

■ Being a good neighbor

All organizations should try to distill the essence of their mission as clearly and briefly as possible. And they should be honest. The mission statement should be forward-looking, but not looking forward into a fantasy world.

Can a quality policy serve the same purpose as a mission statement? After all, all organizations with ISO 9001 systems have a quality policy. The answer is maybe. If the organization takes a broad view of what the term "quality" can mean, then the quality policy might address many or all of the concerns of a mission statement. However, most organizations take a somewhat narrower view of the issues when writing their quality policies.

It's worth examining your own organization's mission statement (if one exists) and determining if it accurately reflects what you know to be the organization's purpose, intentions, and values. Is it simply written? Is it brief, no more than 200 words?

Strategy picks up where mission leaves off. The mission provides high-level themes; strategy gets specific. Strategy puts legs on the mission. It covers a significant period of time, usually a year or more, and describes the broad actions that will be necessary for the organization to fulfill the mission. In a sense, strategy is the battle plan for the war that the mission statement declares.

A clearly defined strategy might address many of the following issues:

■ Competitive angle (e.g., We will compete on the basis of quality, not short lead time.)

■ The means of growth and/or survival (e.g., We plan to acquire one of our competitors in the next year.)

■ Changes in the product offering (e.g., We will launch a new line of products.)

■ Pricing policies (e.g., We will discount our low-end product line to compete directly with foreign imports.)

■ Marketing techniques (e.g., We will begin marketing through an interactive Web site.)

■ Partnerships and alliances (e.g., We will form a joint venture with a Chinese company for manufacturing spare parts.)

■ Relationships in the larger community (e.g., We will build a Habitat for Humanity home in the adjoining town.)

■ Inventory quantities (e.g., We will begin reducing inventory in stock throughout all warehouses.)

■ Production capabilities (e.g., We will acquire the capability to fulfill an order in five days or fewer.)

■ Human resource competencies (e.g., We must improve the literacy rate of our employees because it's beginning to affect the quality of our output.)

■ General staffing levels (e.g., We must increase our sales force.)

■ Technological requirements (e.g., We must learn to service this new line of computers.)

■ Process requirements (e.g., We must develop processes for washing all parts when they arrive in our facilities.)

■ Logistics and transportation (e.g., We will discontinue our own fleet of trucks and begin outsourcing the transportation of outbound freight.)

■ Effects on the environment (e.g., We must reduce contaminants going into storm water runoff.)

■ Changes expected within the competitive environment (e.g., The local technical college will close next year, and this will hamper our ability to train employees.)

Strategy can cover nearly any issue that's important to an organization, and obviously issues might differ drastically from one company to the next. Consider our fictional Yellowjacket Technologies. The executive managers locked themselves in the conference room for two days (surviving on beluga caviar and Kentucky bourbon) and came up with the following strategic plan:

YELLOWJACKET TECHNOLOGIES STRATEGIC PLAN

Strategic imperatives

■ Maintain prominence in new-product development

■ Regain market share in stock lines

■ Retain skilled employees

■ Rationalize overall cost structure to build profits

Current outlook

■ We're seen as the undisputed leader in innovation.

■ Nakisako Ltd. is chipping away at our market share in some product lines—due particularly to reliability problems (see item below).

■ Reliability of electronic components has eroded.

■ Workforce is motivated and engaged in our mission.

■ Inventories of K- and H-line products are moving very slowly; Southside warehouse is at capacity.

■ Profits have fallen during the past two quarters.

Strategy

■ Design breakthrough product configurations

■ Continue supporting HR initiatives to maintain a motivated workforce

■ Improve reliability of components and final assemblies

■ Reduce inventories of slow-moving products

■ Examine cost-cutting opportunities to improve profits

■ Improve overall customer ratings to shield encroachment from competitors

■ Continue building our reputation as a good neighbor

Action plans

■ Develop and begin marketing three new products in top product line by end of year.
(Responsibility: A. Nelson)

■ Design and implement formal employee suggestion system within the first quarter.
(Responsibility: J. Sanchez)

■ Reduce production costs by 5 percent through employee suggestion system.
(Responsibility: J. Sanchez)

■ Improve reliability of components and final assemblies by at least 30 percent.
(Responsibility: T. Fujiki)

■ Reduce inventories of slow-moving parts to fewer than 30 days in stock.
(Responsibility: H. Atkins)

■ Reduce inventories of all parts to fewer than 45 days in stock.
(Responsibility: H. Atkins)

■ Enter into long-term contracts with commodity suppliers (e.g., packaging, transportation and electronic components) to reduce costs.
(Responsibility: B. Wilson)

■ Conduct second round of customer field reports, with a target of 20 percent improvement of overall scores from previous year.
(Responsibility: R. Wiley)

■ Begin construction on Habitat for Humanity house in adjoining community. Target completion for November/December time frame.
(Responsibility: P. Chiappina)

With clear and concise strategy and mission statements, developing key measures becomes relatively easy. In fact, some key measures are written right into the action plan shown above. Some of the measurable, high-level objectives that could be taken directly from it include:

■ Net income
■ Days of inventory on hand
■ Failure rate of key products
■ Average unit cost
■ Customer satisfaction index

Key measures put strategy into language that everyone can understand. They boil complex topics into simple charts and graphs that almost anyone can interpret at a glance, and they give everyone in the organization something to shoot for. When you explain to employees what "average unit cost" means, why it's important, and what each person can do to improve this number, you create an army of people dedicated to helping the organization achieve its strategy. What could be more powerful?

Obviously, not all employees will be able to contribute to every key measure, but they'll be able to contribute to at least one or two. The trick is to balance the portfolio so that the key measures are broad enough to address concerns that all personnel can work toward. Some of this can be achieved through lower-level objectives, a topic that will be addressed in the next chapter.

Well-conceived mission and strategy statements make selecting key measures easy. Get your arms around mission and strategy, and you're basically there. The only hitch is that mission and strategy sometimes don't serve the purpose they're intended to serve. Sometimes they don't even exist.

PROBLEMS WITH MISSION AND STRATEGY

Organizations aren't perfect. Often they fumble around and survive only because the winds of fortune happen to be blowing in their direction. They might be alive today, but don't bet too much money on tomorrow. It's a challenge to select key measures in these sorts of organizations. Consider these three scenarios:

■ *Undefined mission and strategy.* A common problem is that an organization hasn't bothered to define its mission and strategy clearly. Top management isn't necessarily at fault here. Determining mission and strategy takes time and energy, and sometimes top management is consumed by today's crisis (which, of course, occurs on a daily basis). "Mission and strategy? Are you crazy? We've got twenty orders that must ship this afternoon!" The organization slugs it out every day, just trying to keep its head above the flood waters, and the process of planning for the future never happens.

■ *Mission and strategy are not understood throughout the organization.* This scenario is probably the most common. A mission statement was conceived, even written down somewhere. Likewise, strategy was drawn up. Top managers probably hired a consultant, spent a few days at a mountain or beach retreat, and dined their way through strategic planning. When everyone returned, the strategy was promptly filed away in a desk drawer and never looked at again. Even in organizations that actually manage to develop their strategies, it's usually only done at the highest levels. Personnel below the top rung often have little understanding of how they can advance strategy on a practical level.

■ *Mission and strategy don't reflect reality.* Sometimes members of organizations fool themselves. They believe a threat exists where one doesn't and completely ignore what any child could identify as looming disaster. They forgo huge opportunities in favor of more risky ventures. They believe their customers are thrilled when, in truth, they're about to become as rare as Sasquatch sightings in New York City. In organizations led by a powerful and domineering chief executive, and where relative weakness exists among the other key players, mission and strategy sometimes fail to reflect reality. In this scenario, mission and strategy conceivably could guide the development of key measures, but they would be the wrong key measures.

In each of these cases, it might seem as if developing key measures is an insurmountable task. It's not. A tool called the key measures selection worksheet, explained in the next section, will assist any organization in developing a set of strategic key measures. Even excellent organizations should utilize it to confirm their logic and validate their strategic planning process.

THE KEY MEASURES SELECTION WORKSHEET

The worksheet, which is shown on page 27 at the end of this chapter, provides a structured approach to developing key measures. It attempts to get past everyone's mental baggage about what's really important in the organization and leads participants through a fresh exploration of the variables of success. Without a tool of this sort, management often ends up using the following for key measures:

■ *Measures they've always used.* Typically these are traditional accounting measures, which only reveal a portion of the organization's future.

■ *Measures they're comfortable with.* These might not have any bearing whatsoever on the organization's long-term survival. The best measures often make people uncomfortable because they reveal the true state of affairs.

The key measures worksheet helps everyone to focus on what really affects the organization's success and survival, and prevents key measures from drifting toward the realm of "what we've always measured" and "what we feel most comfortable measuring." Sometimes these types of measures do constitute key measures, but it's critical to consider the full range of possible measures.

The organization's top managers should be asked to complete the key measures selection worksheet individually; then the results can be discussed in a group format. Who constitutes "top management" really depends on the organizational unit that's trying to develop key measures. If this is for an entire corporation, then top management will probably consist of the CEO, vice presidents, and other big bananas. If key measures are being developed for a plant or an office, top management might consist of the general manager, director of operations, customer service supervisor, and similar personnel. The trick is to involve diverse participants so that the results aren't overly homogeneous. Remember, key measures should reflect the full range of organizational concerns bearing on success; one particular function can't dominate.

Completing the key measures selection worksheet generally takes 30 minutes to an hour for individuals, then another 30 minutes to an hour to discuss the results as a group. So plan on the initial exercise taking about two hours. Whoever facilitates the session should complete a key measures selection worksheet on his or her own, just to get an idea of what the results might reveal. Here's the recommended procedure for facilitating the key measures selection worksheet in a group setting:

- *Bring top managers together to complete the worksheet.* Let them know ahead of time what will be expected and the time required. Having lunch provided as part of the exercise seems to help in some cases. It's also helpful if the most senior manager begins the session by saying a few words about the importance of the continual improvement process and how key measures will help get everyone concentrated on the real drivers of success. Then each manager will complete the worksheet individually.
- *Gain consensus on draft measures.* After everyone has completed his or her own worksheet, the facilitator will lead group discussion of what each participant came up with for each of the draft key measures in turn. The facilitator should encourage a free flow of discussion, while keeping everyone

focused on key measures. Use a flip chart to record the draft key measures. As the discussion winds down, get consensus from the group on what the draft measures will be. Between four and eight key measures is usually the most effective number.

■ *Allow participants time to think about draft measures.* It's important to allow all the participants some time to think about the draft key measures away from the group. Set a date for reconvening the group and ask that all participants think about the draft measures on their own. Explain that when the group reconvenes, they'll commit to the final key measures. It's helpful to send out the draft key measures in memo or e-mail form to all the participants immediately after the meeting. And make sure to send out a reminder about the next meeting.

■ *Reconvene the group to decide on the final key measures.* On the appointed day, gather the top managers back together to determine the key measures. Get all participants' buy-in on each measure because these are what the organization will be managing by in the future. Finally, make sure that everyone understands that the key measures process isn't an exact science; it's your best guess at what matters the most. There might be a wide range of measures that could reflect the strategic success or failure of the organization.

DEFINING KEY MEASURES

Terms such as "productivity," "efficiency," "utilization," and even "cost" have very different meanings to different people. In fact, the words have almost no value unless they're clearly defined. Make no assumptions about the clarity of a word or concept: Nail it down.

A number of elements should be included in each key measure's definition. These include the following:

■ *What exactly is being measured?* Efficiency, for instance, measures "how well inputs are turned into outputs." You could also say that efficiency measures "the percentage of raw materials that get converted to final products." Both these definitions help to clarify the purpose and significance of the measure. Technical buzzwords, on the other hand, aren't helpful to anybody.

■ *What's the measure's link to mission and strategy?* This is helpful in establishing the measure's relevance in relation to the organization's reason for existence. Of course, this is only applicable if the organization has documented its mission and strategy.

■ *How is the objective calculated?* This is critical yet nearly always over-looked. "Heck, everyone around here knows how we calculate productivi-ty!" No, actually, everyone doesn't. Spell out the calculation in terms that would allow someone to do the math.

■ *What's the data source?* Data can come from multiple—and sometimes con-flicting—sources. Determine the official data source for each key measure.

■ *How often are data collected?* The frequency of data collection is an impor-tant variable to the process. Another consideration is what time of the month (or week or year) the data are collected because timing can often influence the data.

■ *Who collects the data and generates charts?* Exactly who will collect the data is another significant, yet often forgotten, detail related to metrics. Assign someone as the custodian of each key measure. This person will col-lect the data at the appointed time, perform whatever calculations are nec-essary, and produce the graphics that make the data understandable at a glance. Convert raw data to graphics whenever possible.

■ *How is progress on the measure communicated to the organization?* This detail will often be developed over time as the continual improvement sys-tem evolves. However, communication methods must at least be considered at the beginning of the system. Most organizations are media heavy these days, so communication shouldn't be much of a problem.

■ *How is the measure formally reviewed?* Finally, the organization must decide exactly how key measures will be reviewed by top management and how they'll be used as a guide to actions and decisions. Timing of the review process is also a consideration.

It's categorically impossible to provide too much definition on key meas-ures. Define the measure in plain language so that anybody can understand it.

The key measure definitions worksheet, shown on page 30 at the end of this chapter, is for recording these definitional details. The worksheet's output can provide the input to official documentation related to the key measures. For that matter, the worksheet itself could become the formal key measures documentation, but most organizations choose to document these issues in a more formal manner.

Note that if the key measure definitions worksheet proves impossible to complete, then there's a good chance that the so-called key measure in ques-tion isn't actually measurable.

From time to time, managers will utter flowery nonsense and declare that it constitutes a key measure. This is a mistake that's easy to correct. You'll know flowery nonsense when you hear it. Some examples are:

■ Build the kind of organization that nurtures the creative spirit and innate genius of each individual within these walls

■ Achieve a wow factor that's off the scale in the hearts and minds of our many valued customers

■ Crush our competitors with the heels of my great jackboots

These might all be admirable concepts. In an abstract way, they can even be pursued. They need further clarification, however, before we can measure the organization's progress toward their achievement.

When faced with flowery nonsense, ask, "What will indicate whether we're achieving that objective?" If the answer is concrete, measurable, and linked to the organization's strategy, you might have your key measure.

DOCUMENTING KEY MEASURES

Documentation simply means that the key measures have been formalized to facilitate their communication. It's absolutely essential. Formal documentation typically involves a few easy steps:

■ *Putting the key measures in a fixed form that's readily understandable and accessible.* What constitutes "readily understandable and accessible" will differ from one organization to another. It could be a traditional text-based paper document, a graphical representation, or electronic media of some sort. Don't get too hung up on how the key measures should be documented—just document them. If the form of documentation you chose doesn't work that well, switch to a different one.

■ *Approving the key measures before use.* Approval signifies that the key measures have been approved by the appropriate authorities. It gives the measures credibility and underlines their significance.

■ *Clearly displaying the revision status.* Revision status allows those who use the key measures (i.e., everybody in the organization) to know that they have the most current version. This is typically demonstrated through a date, revision number, or revision letter. The revision status typically ties back to some central list or index that indicates which revision is the most current.

There are other controls that can be applied to documentation, but the ones shown above are probably the most critical. If your organization has a document control system such as those that are required by ISO 9001 or other management system models, then the key measures can easily be incorporated into the normal control protocols.

Managers occasionally bristle at the idea of documenting their key measures. (Actually, they bristle at the idea of documenting anything.) Documentation is critical to consistently communicating key measures to everyone in the organization. As we'll see in the next chapter, nothing happens on key measures without effective communication.

CONNECTION TO ISO 9001

You might wonder how key measures relate to ISO 9001 requirements, particularly the one for so-called "quality objectives." The good news is that there's a direct relationship. The key measures will become your quality objectives within the ISO 9001 system, as illustrated in Figure 2.1.

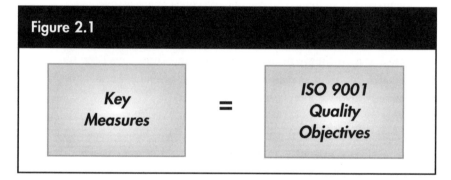

Figure 2.1

Key Measures = ISO 9001 Quality Objectives

It doesn't matter that the key measures are more strategic and global than what would normally be expected with something as narrowly defined as quality objectives. In fact, that's a good thing. This gives the ISO 9001 system a needed boost and reinforces its role as a strategic management tool. It's strongly recommended that ISO 9001-registered organizations don't even use the term "quality objectives." It has very narrow connotations and can give the impression that objectives are only relevant to part of the organization. Call your measurable objectives within the ISO 9001 system key measures, business objectives, company goals—anything but quality objectives.

DOS AND DON'TS OF SELECTING KEY MEASURES

Keep the following issues in mind when your organization begins studying its mission and strategy and selecting key measures:

✔ *Do sell top management on key measures.* Before doing anything, make sure top management buys into key measures as a tool for decision making and communicating strategy throughout the organization. If top management doesn't believe in the process, it won't go anywhere.

✔ *Do benchmark other organizations.* Many other organizations have adopted the concept of key measures as a primary tool for driving continual improvement. They might not call them key measures, but the concept is the same. Do some networking and find out what kind of metrics these organizations are using. What has worked well for them and what hasn't? Unless they are head-to-head competitors of yours, most organizations will be happy to share this type of information.

✔ *Do clearly define key measures.* Spell out every possible detail related to each key measure so there's no room for confusion or misinterpretation. Use the key measures definition worksheet to help clarify all the facets.

✔ *Do document key measures.* Documentation of some form is the only sure way to ensure that everyone gets the same message about the key measures.

✔ *Do convert the data to graphics.* Key measures that result in variable data should always be depicted in a graphic manner—the simpler the better. Nothing tells a story better than a picture.

✔ *Do get creative.* Invent your own measures, if necessary. Existing indicators might not capture the performance variables that matter most to your organization. If you do adequate benchmarking, though, you probably won't have to get too creative.

✔ *Do include customer perception metrics.* The single most important metric an organization can have is what its customers think about the organization. Everything else is secondary to this. Make sure that at least one key measure is directly related to customer satisfaction.

✘ *Don't select too many key measures.* Most organizations will end up with no more than eight to ten key measures at the very most. The power of key measures lies in their ability to focus everyone on the few issues that really matter. Keep the list tight.

✘ *Don't select key measures without facilitation.* Even the savviest leaders need help when selecting key measures. This avoids the mental traps and paradigms that managers fall victim to. The key measures selection worksheet is an invaluable tool for facilitating the selection of key measures.

✗ *Don't focus too much on accounting measures.* There's no way around the fact that accounting and financial measures are important. The problem is that they're always backward-looking and don't tell much about the future. Strike a balance between accounting measures and other metrics that reveal performance on a variety of organizational fronts and across different time frames.

✗ *Don't neglect important attribute measures.* We talk so much about variable measures that it's easy to forget that attribute measures can be just as strategic. If projects have strategic importance, combined with clear deliverables and due dates, then they easily qualify as key measures. An example might be, "Hire and train three new salespeople with backgrounds in industrial electronics by June 15." Depending on your strategy and competitive environment, this might be the most important measure in your portfolio.

Now that you've defined and documented the organization's key measures, you must tell everybody what they mean. Communicating key measures is the subject of chapter three.

Chapter Two Appendix

SAMPLE KEY MEASURES

What follows is a sampling of key measures. They only represent a small fraction of the possible universe of measures that could be considered "key."

Revenue

Other names: sales, proceeds, funding, inflows, receipts, top line, billings, collections

What does it measure? Revenue reflects the organization's ability to attract funds for its goods, services, or activities. All organizations rely on some sort of revenue for their existence. Even churches, charities, clubs, and the federal government depend on revenue for survival, but the revenue often goes by a different name (e.g., offerings, donations, dues, taxes). For business organizations, revenue is the first step toward realizing a profit.

A decline in revenues could indicate decreasing demand for the organization's products, strengthening of competitors, a declining economy, or other problems. It's important to recognize that revenues within accrual accounting systems don't necessarily equal cash receipts; sales are counted as revenue during the period they're booked, despite the fact money might not have actually changed hands.

Calculation: Revenue = (cash receipts + receivables) − (returns + discounts + allowances)

Strengths:
- Strong relevance to nearly all human organizations
- The concept is readily understandable.
- Data are already available within typical business accounting systems.

Weaknesses:
- Revenues might differ significantly from actual cash receipts.
- Doesn't indicate how well the organization manages its costs
- Owners of privately held businesses might be reluctant to share this kind of information.

Profit

Other names: net income, earnings, bottom line

What does it measure? Profit indicates the organization's ability to manage its operations in such a way that revenues exceed costs. Theoretically, profits are the funds that are left at the end of the period when all sales have been booked and all expenses tallied. All organizations must concern themselves with managing revenues vs. expenses; thus, profit is a universal concept.

A decline in profits might indicate that the organization isn't controlling its costs or managing its resources effectively, or it could indicate that revenues have fallen. Like revenue, the calculation for profit within accrual accounting systems utilizes transactions that aren't true exchanges of money. For this reason, "profit" and actual cash remaining at the end of the period might not be equal.

Calculation: Profit = revenues – (expenses + interest payments + depreciation + taxes)

Strengths:
- Strong relevance to all business organizations
- The concept is readily understandable.
- Data are already available within typical business accounting systems.

Weaknesses:
- Profit might differ significantly from cash remaining at the end of the period.
- Profit is often a poor indicator of performance for small and/or start-up organizations because cash is critical to their survival.
- Owners of privately held businesses might be reluctant to share this kind of information.

Cash flow

Other names: money, currency, green

What does it measure? Cash flow is similar to profit except that it considers only cash that actually enters and leaves the organization. It doesn't recognize receivables, payables, and depreciation, which aren't cash transactions. Cash flow is a much more honest measure of an organization's financial health.

Calculation: Cash flow = cash revenues – (cash expenses + interest payments + taxes)

Strengths:
- Has profound bearing on the life or death of the organization
- Provides a quick sanity check against accounting results
- Can provide an early warning for disaster
- The concept is readily understandable.

Weaknesses:

■ Data collection systems might not exist.

■ Owners of privately held businesses might be reluctant to share this kind of information.

Percent perfect orders

This is a relatively unique measure that combines a number of different performance indicators into a single composite metric. The basic premise is that the organization wants as many of its orders and/or transactions to be as perfect as possible from the customer's perspective. What constitutes a perfect order will vary from organization to organization, but generally it follows these guidelines:

■ No complaints

■ Order arrived on time or service was performed on time

■ No charge backs

■ No credits

■ No billing errors

■ No negotiated changes in the order due to problems on the organization's end

■ Payment was received from customer on time

Remember that any of the problems listed above keep an order from being considered perfect.

Calculation: Percent perfect orders = Perfect orders during period/Total orders during same period

Strengths:

■ Focuses on performance from the customer's perspective

■ Provides a single number that everyone can concentrate on

■ Forward-looking; success against this measure can help ensure long-term success

■ Components of the measure (e.g., complaints and late orders) can be analyzed individually.

■ The overall concept is readily understandable.

Weaknesses:

■ Data collection systems might not exist.

■ Data most likely will come from different sources and coordinating data can be difficult.

Inventory turnover

Other names or similar concepts: stock churn, days of inventory on hand (the inverse of inventory turnover)

What does it measure? Organizations that produce goods that go into inventory typically are concerned with how long the goods stay in inventory. The less time, the better. Inventory is treated as an asset by accounting systems, but the reality is that it's often a liability. Inventory is subject to damage, obsolescence, and costs of storage and movement. Inventory also ties up capital that could be used for other purposes. Smart organizations strive for their inventory to "turn over" as many times per year as possible.

Calculation: Number of inventory turns = Cost of goods sold/Inventory value (or average inventory value)

This formula works because it takes the total cost of goods sold for a period and divides it by the current inventory. This gives an idea of how fast the inventory is turning over. Many other formulas for inventory turnover exist, but in all cases the numerator and denominator in the calculation must be in the same units.

Strengths:
■ Can reveal the effectiveness of the organization's production management and sales forecasting systems
■ Highlights costs that are often neglected or ignored
■ Increase in inventory turnover can improve cash flow.
■ Production processes typically become leaner and more efficient as a byproduct of improving inventory turnover.

Weaknesses:
■ Data collection systems might have to be developed.
■ Difficult to apply to service organizations

Employee turnover

Other names: organizational attrition

Organizations might want their inventory to turn over but not their employees. When an employee leaves the organization, the organization bears the cost of screening, interviewing, hiring, orienting, and training a new person, not to mention the loss in productivity that typically accompanies a new hire during the first few months. These costs can be huge, especially when highly skilled and experienced people leave. Just like inventory turnover, the costs of employee turnover aren't captured by most financial accounting systems.

(Note: the term "employee" can be expanded to mean organizational member, thus making this metric applicable to any type of organization.)

Calculation: Employee turnover = Number of employees lost during the period/Total number of employees at the start of the period

The number of employees lost should include employees lost for any reason: fired, quit, laid-off, disabled, or job-related deaths. The only numbers not included are deaths from natural causes because the organization typically isn't able to influence this number. This metric can also be calculated on a rolling twelve-month basis.

Strengths:

- Forward-looking; success against this measure can help ensure long-term success
- Highlights costs that often are neglected or ignored
- Can reveal the effectiveness of the organization's systems for screening, selecting, training, and managing personnel
- Reduction in employee turnover can improve cash flow
- Focuses on the most important resource possessed by most organizations: their people
- Very easy to calculate and understand

Weaknesses:

- Data collection systems might have to be developed.

Efficiency

Other names: organizational competence, input/output ratio, conversion rate

What does it measure? Efficiency indicates how well an organization uses inputs to produce outputs. It's typically expressed as a percentage, which indicates the proportion of inputs that successfully get converted to outputs. An organization with high efficiency converts the majority of its inputs (e.g., raw material, energy, or hours) into products. An organization with lower efficiency loses or wastes more of its inputs during the transformation process. Efficiency is a very typical metric for manufacturing organizations, but it can also be calculated for service providers.

Calculation: Efficiency = inputs/outputs

Both the numerator and denominator in the calculation must be in the same units, such as pounds, dollars, or units. It's very important with efficiency calculations to state exactly what constitutes the source of data for inputs and outputs because there are often multiple sources for both.

Strengths:

■ Focuses on the product realization process, which is the heart of most business organizations

■ Easily understood by production personnel

■ Can highlight problems with internal defects, scrap, and rework, which sometimes get neglected

■ Can highlight supplier problems

■ Directly controllable by production personnel

Weaknesses:

■ Data collection systems might have to be developed.

■ Doesn't reveal whether products were sold

Figure 2.2: Key Measures Selection Worksheet

Completed by: _____

_____

Name of organization: _____ Date: ___/___/___

Section One

1.1. Type of organization:

❑ Manufacturing ❑ Service (select one)

❑ Privately owned ❑ Public (select one)

1.2. Primary customer(s):

_____

1.3. Primary material input(s):

_____

Supplier(s): _____

1.4. Primary nonmaterial input(s):

_____

Supplier(s): _____

Section Two

2.1. Source of competitive advantage:

_____

2.2. "Why should I buy your product instead of the competitor's?" (Be very specific):

_____

2.3. What do we value the most about our organization?

_____

2.4. What was our biggest success last year?

_____

2.5. What's the one thing that makes me most proud about being employed here?

_____

Section Three

3.1. What was the top customer complaint last year?

_____

3.2. What's our biggest general weakness?

_____

3.3. Day in and day out, what keeps us from getting our work done?

_____

3.4. What makes me most frustrated at work?

3.5. What do shareholders or stakeholders worry about the most?

Section Four

4.1. In what direction is the industry headed?

4.2. Where do we think the growth will be during the next three years?

4.3. What will make us (or keep us) the leader during the next three years?

4.4. What's our most promising opportunity?

Section Five

5.1. What could destroy us in the future if we're not careful?

5.2. Who is our biggest competitor?

5.3. What do customers like about this competitor?

5.4. What product or company, while not currently competing against us, could go head to head with us in the future?

5.5. Our biggest scare of the last year was this:

Section Six: Narrowing Our Focus

6.1. From section two, what seems to emerge as our biggest strength(s)? List up to two strengths:

6.2. What would serve as an effective measure of this strength(s)?

6.3. Are there any especially important accounting and/or finance measures that relate to this strength(s)?

6.4. How about nonfinancial measures?

6.5. From section three, what are the consistent issues (i.e., problems mentioned more than once)?

6.6. What is our biggest weakness from section three?

6.7. What measure indicates whether we're getting better or worse at the problem from section three that has the greatest potential to hurt us?

6.8. Analyzing section four, where does it look like we should be headed?

6.9. What measures our movement in this direction?

6.10. From section five, what catches your eye?

6.11. Imagine you're on the board of directors. What issue from section five scares you the most?

6.12. What measure indicates whether or not we have control of this scariest issue?

Section Seven: Draft Key Measures

Rewrite the measures from the respective sections above. These will be your draft key measures and will get you started into the continual improvement process:

Measure from 6.3:

Measure from 6.4:

Measure from 6.7:

Measure from 6.9:

Measure from 6.12:

Figure 2.3: Key Measure Definitions Worksheet

Date: ___/___/___ Completed by: _____

Complete all spaces below:

1. Name of key measure:

2. What exactly does this measure?

3. Link to mission:

4. Link to strategy:

5. Calculation used to arrive at measure:

6. Source of data:

7. Frequency of data collection:

8. Timing of data collection:

9. Who collects data?

10. Who generates charts (if applicable)?

11. Method(s) of communicating progress to organization:

12. Formal review forum:

Approved by: _____ Title: _____

Date: ___/___/___

Chapter Three

Communicating What's Important

In This Chapter
- Educate Midlevel Managers
- Identify Local Activities
- Roll Out Key Measures
- Continuous Communication

Selecting key measures might seem like a significant milestone. It is, but the real work hasn't even started yet. Now that your organization has decided what's important, it must communicate the key measures thoroughly so that they are understood from one corner of the organization to the other. Companies are good at many things, but internal communication often isn't one of them. For this reason, communicating key measures must be carefully planned and executed in phases.

PHASE ONE: EDUCATE MIDLEVEL MANAGERS

The first phase of communication will be directed to departmental and/or process managers. These are what most people consider to be "in the trench" managers, such as production managers, warehouse foremen, or customer service supervisors. Managers working in the trench are generally those who supervise the lion's share of work within the organization. They need to hear the details of the key measures first because they will probably have to handle the most questions about them. "How do we contribute to average unit cost in this process?" "Should I spend less time on the phone with my customers because we're trying to reduce cycle time?" "Why is inventory turnover important?" Managers must have the answers to these questions if their people are expected to contribute to the effort.

A staff meeting is often effective for communicating to managers. A face-to-face meeting as opposed to a memo, e-mail, or voice message will allow for active dialogue and questions. The meeting should cover:

■ Key measures explained in detail
■ The reason why each measure is considered "key"
■ The fact that the measures will be used for decision making and management, and that the managers will be an important part of the process

It's helpful if a printed version of these details is provided during the meeting to cut down on the errors that will inevitably result when people try to take notes. The meeting should take as long as is needed. Don't arbitrarily end the meeting after an hour just because someone thinks that's how long the meeting should last. Take as long as needed to answer all the questions that might arise. These managers are the people who probably will have the most effect on key measures on a daily basis, so all concerns and questions must be addressed.

PHASE TWO: IDENTIFY LOCAL ACTIVITIES AFFECTING KEY MEASURES

Don't even think about communicating key measures to the organization as a whole until all managers understand what activities in their areas contribute to the measures' achievement. Some managers will understand immediately how activities within their areas contribute, but others will find themselves baffled. If the key measures were chosen in a balanced and strategic manner, there should be at least one key measure to which each department or process can contribute. The departments might not be able to gauge the key measure directly in their processes, but they'll be able to contribute to it in some way. The trick is for the managers to "translate" the key measures into concepts that relate directly to the work they're responsible for managing.

The key measures translation worksheet, shown in Figure 3.1 on page 33, will assist in the process. Each manager should assemble a small group of his or her most trusted lieutenants and go over each of the items on the worksheet. One worksheet is completed for each key measure. The session could be handled as a brainstorming event or simply as a discussion. The line of questioning is very simple:

■ *What activities and/or behaviors in our process will help improve this key measure? Who should carry out these activities and/or behaviors?* This is

Figure 3.1: Key Measure Translation Worksheet

To be completed on the departmental or process level for each key measure.

Key Measure:_____

1. What activities and/or behaviors in our process will help improve this key measure? Who should carry out these activities and/or behaviors?

What	Who
_____	_____
_____	_____
_____	_____
_____	_____
_____	_____
_____	_____
_____	_____
_____	_____
_____	_____

2. Are there any measures we can track in our process that indicate whether any of the activities or behaviors listed above are successful?

❏ Yes   ❏ No

If yes, please list the measures:

_____
_____
_____
_____
_____
_____
_____
_____
_____
_____
_____
_____
_____

Completed by:_____ Date: ___/___/___

where the department and/or process translates the key measures into tasks that it can act upon daily. In some ways, this might be the most important step in the entire process of strategic continual improvement. We're taking the abstract concepts of the key measures and turning them into something specific and actionable on the process level. This takes any potential confusion or mystery out of each key measure.

■ *Are there any measures we can track in our process that indicate whether the activities or behaviors listed above are successful?* Sometimes departments and/or processes can track lower-level measures that indicate whether progress has occurred. As an example, it might be very difficult, if not impossible, for the shipping department to track net income using data from their department. But it certainly can track the percentage of late orders and the number of damaged shipments, both of which could have a direct effect on net income from a cost standpoint. However, departments shouldn't track lower-level measures simply for the sake of papering their walls with charts; it should be done only when significant activities in the area strongly link to key measures.

Departments should be given a reasonable time frame within which to complete the key measure translation worksheet for each measure. A couple of weeks should be adequate. Once all departments and/or processes have completed their worksheets, the organization is ready for full deployment of key measures throughout the organization.

PHASE THREE: ROLL OUT KEY MEASURES TO ENTIRE ORGANIZATION

The two preceding steps have laid the foundation for fully deploying the key measures. If the previous steps have been performed correctly, then this third step will be relatively easy. It only becomes difficult when one of the earlier steps have been short-circuited.

The rollout phase is actually composed of two substeps:

■ An organizationwide meeting hosted by the chief executive
■ Departmental meetings that directly follow the organizationwide meeting

The first meeting emphasizes the significance of the key measures. This meeting should convey the big picture of the organization and its competitive environment. This meeting's specific content is nearly the same as the earlier meeting involving the managers:

■ Key measures explained in detail

■ The reason why each measure is considered "key"

■ The fact that the measures will be used for decision making and management, and that everyone in the organization will be part of the process

There are two differences between this meeting and the earlier meeting with managers. One is that the organizationwide meeting can't be an open-ended affair. Due to the nature of pulling everyone away from his or her normal activities, you can only allow for finite number of questions and concerns. Handle the questions that are put forth in the allowed time (generally sixty to ninety minutes), then direct everyone to ask additional questions during the departmental meetings that will directly follow the present meeting. The other difference is that the organizationwide meeting can be virtual—a teleconference, for example—as opposed to a physical gathering. With very large and far-flung organizations, a virtual meeting of some sort is almost a necessity.

Immediately following the organizationwide meeting, participants will split into the departmental meetings. These are best handled as true face-to-face gatherings. This is where the detailed questions will be asked about how the department or function can contribute to key measures. Having gone through this thought process while completing the key measure translation worksheet, the departmental or functional managers will have specific examples of how their personnel can contribute to key measures and supporting measures.

All departmental meeting participants should leave the gathering with a basic understanding of why the key measures are important and what actions and behaviors will lead to their achievement. Forklift drivers will understand how they contribute to key measures as they move product on their forklifts. Customer service reps will understand how they contribute when they pick up the telephone. The billing clerk will understand how preparing invoices affects key measures. These understandings will be reinforced during the weeks and months ahead as the organization begins to use key measures for decision making and continual improvement.

PHASE FOUR: CONTINUOUS COMMUNICATION

The initial wave of communication is primarily aimed at avoiding the suspicion, confusion, and chaos that often accompanies new organizational initiatives such as introducing key measures. Deep understanding of the measures only comes with time. After the initial wave of communication, the organization must build upon everyone's understanding by establishing an ongoing dialogue about the key measures. Charts and simple graphics illustrating the progress made toward achieving key measures must be visible throughout the organization. Key measures must become part of any gathering on operational performance, whether formal or informal. The goal is to make discussing key measures as common as discussing a big ball game or recent movie. This state of saturation is only achievable when the organization's leaders make key measures the topic of choice in their own conversations. When top managers start caring and talking about something, a magical thing happens: Everyone else begins caring and talking about the same thing.

Modes of communication are almost limitless. The trick is to match the type of communication to the audience. One type of communication might be effective in one organization but not in another. Here are a few of the many different communication modes organizations can use:

■ Departmental meetings, staff meetings, shift meetings
■ Memos
■ Bulletin board postings
■ Voice-mail messages
■ E-mails
■ Letters mailed to employees' homes
■ Intranet and Internet site postings
■ Newsletter articles
■ Short videos
■ Games at organizational events such as picnics, open houses, or holiday parties

Simplicity is often the key to effective communication. And, as always, pictures can convey more meaning to most people than words can.

One of the themes these communications should stress is the actions the organization is taking to improve key measures. All kinds of actions: strategic, tactical, big, little, global, localized. When people see that key measures are truly motivating decisions and actions throughout the organization, they'll become much more interested in them.

The ability to successfully communicate key measures sets the stage for analysis and action, which is the topic of the next chapter.

Chapter Four

Analysis and Action

In This Chapter
- Top Level Review
- The Basics of Reviewing Data
- Generating Improvement Actions
- Tracking Projects to Completion

We now arrive at a critical juncture in the continual improvement process: analysis and action. These two activities are inseparable. Analysis without action is meaningless. Action without analysis is dangerous. Both activities must work in harmony for the organization to realize any benefit.

Analysis and action can take place nearly anywhere within the organization. Indeed, the more places analysis and action occur, the better. However, the most important place to review key measures for analysis and action is at the top of the organization. Top managers must decide whether current results indicate a movement toward or away from the ultimate organizational objectives of mission and strategy. The key measures will quickly indicate this.

TOP LEVEL REVIEW

Most organizations already hold some sort of regular organizational performance review. These are known by a wide variety of names—monthly wrap-up, close-out meeting, performance roundtable, scorecard assessment, business review, and many others—but they all allow for analysis of the organization's performance and comparison to expectations. Don't invent a new meeting for reviewing key measures; use an existing forum. If the meeting already has credibility and high-level involvement, then the battle is half won. A few revisions to the agenda might be necessary to tailor existing performance reviews to analysis of, and action on, key measures.

The most significant revision is that key measures will be the cornerstone of the performance review. Existing metrics generally will be replaced by key measures. Removing existing metrics often makes managers nervous, but nervous or not, the agenda must change. If existing metrics are critical, they should be formally declared key measures. The only time that this doesn't hold true is when a key measure is composed of other metrics. Profit, for example, is a complicated amalgamation of revenues, costs, investments, and accounting manipulations, so additional data might be necessary to interpret profit trends correctly. However, key measures form the heart of the review.

Reviewing key measures is a tightly focused event, revolving around three primary activities:

■ Analyzing key measures' trends
■ Reviewing actions taken to improve key measures
■ Reviewing organizational warning lights

We should briefly address "organizational warning lights." These are the important intermediate measures that, although not as critical as key measures, still deserve analysis. Examples of organizational warning lights include trends in customer feedback (e.g., complaints, comments, praise, and information from the field and sales channels), corrective and preventive actions, audit results, and product conformity trends. Reviewing this information is valuable and can inform the analysis of key measures. Customer feedback often constitutes a key measure in its own right, but organizations sometimes find measurement of this feedback difficult due to its anecdotal and/or subjective nature.

Organizations registered to ISO 9001 might wonder where that standard's management review fits into all of this. What has been described is the ISO 9001 management review. The key measures, in turn, are the quality objectives required by the standard. This links the ISO 9001 system to strategy-level concerns. The benefits are twofold:

■ ISO 9001 now has a clear connection to strategy. It's no longer just a quality management initiative—it's a strategic management initiative.
■ The system of key measures benefits from the structure and discipline that ISO 9001 offers. Reviews will happen as scheduled, analysis will take place, and actions will be proposed and managed to completion.

If the ISO 9001-based management review becomes separated from the broader review of key measures, then it's doomed to irrelevance. ISO 9001 practitioners must memorize the simple formulas in Figure 4.1, one of which was already presented in chapter two. They're critical to the ongoing survival of the ISO 9001 system.

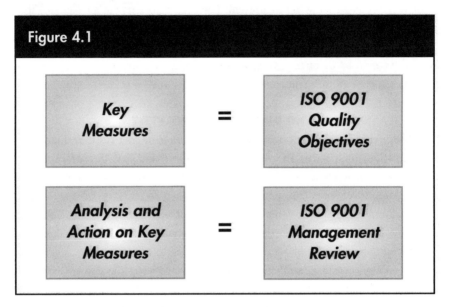

Figure 4.1

| Key Measures | = | ISO 9001 Quality Objectives |
| Analysis and Action on Key Measures | = | ISO 9001 Management Review |

A written procedure is highly recommended to help guide the key measures review. It's not necessary to impose a rigid bureaucracy, just apply lean, simple documentation. The procedure should define the various protocols surrounding the key measures review and ensure that everyone understands the review's goals and his or her role within it. Without guiding documentation, it's easy to let the review become a muddle. A sample procedure for the key measures review and related information is shown in this chapter's appendix, on page 50.

FREQUENCY OF REVIEW

Organizations often struggle with the dilemma of how often they should review key measures. Actually, this isn't much of a dilemma, and it's overcome by answering one simple question: How often is the organization currently reviewing its performance? Most organizations will simply adopt the frequency that's currently employed for performance reviews. Monthly is one of the most prevalent frequencies, for three basic reasons:

■ A month represents a natural delineation of time to many businesspeople.

■ A monthly review matches the reporting frequency of accounting results with most publicly traded companies.

■ Most actions taken to improve key measures won't show results for at least a month, so there's not much point in reviewing progress more often.

Every organization will be different. The trick is to arrive at a frequency that represents the true cycle of planning, action, and results. This might be weekly in some organizations and bimonthly in others. Holding a review of results every six months or once a year, as some organizations claim to do, simply isn't often enough to be meaningful.

WHO SHOULD BE INVOLVED?

Participation in the key measures review must be carefully defined. The organization must strive for wide representation, not just that of executive functions. A group that's too homogeneous will inevitably fall victim to groupthink (i.e., everyone thinking the same way, regardless of the logic). Production, logistics, sales, finance, engineering, and human resources all have valuable perspectives to add to the review. The richer the mix of participants, the richer the analysis and action.

Given key measures' strategic nature, their review must be led by the organization's chief executive. The more involved and plugged in this person is, the more successful the review will be. The chief executive must probe the whys behind key measures trends, and the meeting's participants should have the technical competencies to come up with answers. When the chief executive is intimately engaged in reviewing key measures, the rest of the organization begins to understand how important these metrics are. Interest in improving the measures then flows throughout the organization.

A meeting facilitator is one of the most important roles that can be played during the key measures review. This individual does exactly what you would expect: keeps the review focused and on track. As anyone who has attended meetings knows, they have a way of drifting in unforeseen directions. A facilitator helps to remove distractions and keep the participants concentrated on analysis and action. This individual doesn't act as a heavy-handed dictator but rather a coach who allows all participants to work effectively within the review's scope.

THE BASICS OF REVIEWING DATA

Prior to the review, it's helpful if participants are provided with data about key measures. Receiving selected data a day or two in advance allows participants to begin thinking about the trends and forming some thoughts. This enables them to walk into the meeting fully prepared to discuss the issues. It's also helpful if the data are converted to graphics, both for distribution prior to the review and for analysis during it. Simple graphic tools facilitate the interpretation of raw data. These tools include run charts, bar charts, Pareto diagrams, and pie charts. We're not talking about rocket science here, just converting data into graphic formats. Of course, the raw data on all key measures should be available in case more in-depth analysis is necessary. Raw data tend to add static to the analysis process, so they should be introduced only when truly needed.

Reviewing metrics doesn't come naturally to most managers. It's a subtle process that requires an understanding of the many variables acting on the measures. These variables often dictate whether it is action that's necessary or just continued monitoring of the trends. In particular, review participants must consider these important questions:

■ *What constitutes normal variation vs. a trend that requires action?* Personnel sometimes are anxious to act on every little blip in the data, particularly at the beginning of a continual improvement initiative. However, every little blip isn't statistically significant, and sounding alarms just because a particular index dipped by a point or two can divert everyone's attention from other trends that do have significance. Take action to improve every key measure, but don't treat every upward or downward movement of data as if it has ominous implications. It's worth mentioning that determining statistical significance is impossible without calculating control limits.

■ *Should you be aware of seasonal cycles?* A sled manufacturer will probably see a drop in revenues every summer along with a buildup of inventory. Neither one of these is necessarily a cause for alarm, given the cyclical nature of business for the company.

■ *Are incentives in force that discourage achieving key measures?* It sounds ridiculous that organizations would have incentives that discourage their own objectives, but this is often the case. One example is when personnel receive incentives based on output measures, but the organization as a whole is trying to reduce inventory and/or increase inventory turnover.

TARGET SETTING

Organizations often find it helpful to set targets with their key measures. Targets provide a common, visible goal that motivates action. Here's an example of a key measure with an accompanying target:

Key measure = revenue growth
Target = increase revenue by 3 percent over previous year's levels.

Targets must be set only with an understanding of the variables that influence key measures. For this reason, many organizations find it appropriate to review the measures for a month or two before setting targets. These will then be made based on experience and wisdom about movement of the data.

Targets occasionally have a way of becoming knee-jerk based rather than based on logic and reality. Many organizations are famous for automatically saying, "Two percent better than last year" for every target. Never mind that there's no rational basis for the target; it's one nonetheless. Targets should provide some stretch, but they should be achievable and based in reality. Impossible or arbitrary targets quickly become de-motivators, which is the exact opposite of what they're supposed to be. Actions that will help achieve targets must be clearly defined. Keep in mind that this is the single most important activity that takes place during the key measures review.

It's also worth noting that the target could be written directly into the key measure. It's not necessary that the key measure and its associated target be two separate pieces of information.

GENERATING IMPROVEMENT ACTIONS

Actions must inevitably result from the key measures review. The organization analyzes progress against the key measures and decides upon actions that it believes will drive improvements. Of course, an infinite number of actions exist that the organization could conceivably take. However, resources aren't infinite, and even improvement actions consume resources. The challenge is to generate a wide range of improvement actions, then systematically select the few that will generate the most improvement.

The generation of improvement actions and ideas should take place during the analysis of key measures data. It makes no sense to separate these two functions. In many organizations, measures are reviewed on a high level, then lower levels of the organization are tasked with coming up with ways to improve the measures. This is insanity. If participants in the review function aren't equipped to propose actions to improve the key measures, then the wrong people have been picked to be participants. A good way to ensure improvement inputs is to balance the meeting with a mix of participants representing the full range of functions within the organization.

Improvement actions generated at the organization's highest levels let everyone know how important the measures are. Improvement actions will also be selected at lower levels—at all levels, for that matter—but the process begins at the top.

Generating and selecting improvement actions is a simple process following these steps:

■ Brainstorming actions

■ Prioritizing and selecting the most promising actions by using the improvement needs assessment

■ Implementing actions through project management techniques

These steps are discussed in detail below.

Brainstorming

Most businesspeople have had some experience with brainstorming. It's a simple technique that uses the natural creativity of personnel in a group setting as they play off each other's ideas. The result is a large number of potential actions and initiatives that can improve key measures. The ideas will range from pedestrian to outrageous. Often, the ideas that seem the most outrageous are those that result in the best solutions, either directly or indirectly. That's the power of brainstorming: its ability to expand on the population of ideas, typically in unexpected directions.

The general steps to brainstorming are quite simple:

1. *A facilitator is appointed to lead the brainstorming session.* If a meeting facilitator has already been appointed, then he or she should also facilitate the brainstorming session. If not, someone must be chosen. Facilitating brainstorming is critical; otherwise, chaos can result.

2. *The rules of brainstorming are reviewed with all participants.* Most of the participants will know the rules, but these should be reviewed nonetheless. See the following points for general brainstorming rules and guidelines as they apply to key measures.

3. *Each key measure will be considered in turn.* The facilitator will solicit actions from each of the participants to improve the key measure, recording everyone's ideas on a flipchart or grease board.

4. *Each participant is given a chance to provide input.* The facilitator continues going around the group in a diplomatic manner.

5. *No critiques of the ideas are allowed.* The objective of the process is to encourage everyone's creativity. Outrageous, silly, and facetious inputs are

welcomed. They just might spur someone else into a valuable idea.

6. *Ideas continue to be generated until the group has exhausted itself of creative inputs.*

7. *The next key measure is selected and the brainstorming process begins again.*

Must all improvement actions be aimed directly at key measures? Of course not. Some proposed actions might be completely unrelated to key measures, yet these ideas could provide some of the best opportunities for the organization. This is especially true in lower levels, where drawing a direct connection to key measures is more difficult.

When the group has generated a large number of potential improvement actions, it's time to start prioritizing them.

Prioritizing actions

Every organization, no matter how big or successful, has limited resources. Time, money, space, personnel, equipment, and materials are all constrained. For this reason, organizations don't usually have the luxury of pursuing every single improvement action that's proposed. Even very good ideas for improvement sometimes get dropped. The trick is to systematically prioritize actions so that limited resources are applied to actions that will have the biggest effect on the organization.

There are many ways to prioritize improvement actions that result from a brainstorming session. One of the best is a tool called the improvement needs assessment (shown in this chapter's appendix, on page 53). Improvement needs assessment evaluates each brainstorming output across several dimensions. Some of the dimensions include actions that:

■ Are closely related to key measures—and thus mission and strategy

■ Have a critical internal effect on the organization

■ Aid the customer (such as product improvements or service enhancements)

■ Reduce costs (such as reducing defects or streamlining processes)

■ Have a strong chance of success

Each idea from the brainstorming session is assigned a numeric value for each of the dimensions, according to the guidelines shown on the respective columns of the worksheet. The values in each column are then multiplied by each other going across the column, resulting in a final score for each idea. This provides a quantitative comparison of actions and opportunities, and depersonalizes the process so that feelings don't get hurt.

As an example of how the improvement needs assessment would work, let's say that a hypothetical management team brainstormed activities to improve the key measure of reducing employee turnover. The team produced the following ideas:

- Provide free lunches to employees on Fridays
- Design a training program on practical problem-solving techniques for all employees
- Perform exit interviews with employees at the time that they quit

A real brainstorming session would have produced considerably more than three ideas, but we'll keep the list short for the sake of simplicity. Let's rate the first idea, of providing free lunches to employees on Fridays. You can follow the rating of ideas on the completed improvement needs assessment shown in this chapter's appendix, on page 55.

- *Action linked to key measure?* The group decided that there really wasn't much of a link between free lunches and employee turnover, so a score of one was assigned in this column to represent "no."
- *Action likely to result in cost reductions?* Free lunches would definitely not result in any cost reductions. Indeed, it would raise costs. The group assigned a one to this column to represent "no."
- *Positive effect on employee morale and/or motivation?* This factor generated a great deal of discussion. Some participants believed that free lunches would cause a big boost in employee motivation and morale. Others said that free lunches would only be a motivator in the short term, possibly even becoming a demotivator if employees perceived a decline in the quality of lunches over time (e.g., hot dogs being substituted for steaks). The group struck a compromise and decided that the effect would be "medium," and a score of two was assigned to this column.
- *Importance to customer?* The group decided unanimously that customers couldn't care less if employees got free lunches on Fridays. A score of one was assigned to this column.
- *Importance to internal operations?* After some discussion, the group decided that free lunches probably wouldn't have much positive effect on internal operations. A score of one was assigned to this column.
- *Degree of control over problem or opportunity?* The group decided that the company did have some control over this opportunity, at least on a theoretical level. The only hitch was that some employees might not elect to participate in the free lunches. A two was assigned to this column to represent "medium."

■ *Resources available for implementation?* Due to budgetary constraints, the group decided that the company didn't have the financial resources to provide free lunches (or at least not the kind of free lunches anybody would want to eat). A one was assigned to this column.

The values in each column were multiplied, resulting in a total score of four. Both of the other two ideas were evaluated according to the same criteria. The resulting scores were 243 for the idea of designing a training program on practical problem-solving techniques for all employees, and twenty four for the idea of performing exit interviews on employees at the time that they quit. The results indicate that designing a training program on practical problem-solving techniques for all employees will have the biggest effect on the organization. The participants from the improvement needs assessment share some ownership in the final outcome because their guidance and input affected the scores. This ownership at high levels of the organization helps ensure that the project will be carried to completion.

Another method for prioritizing outputs from a brainstorming session is a technique called multivoting. It's less quantitative than the improvement needs assessment but still leverages the collective experience of the group. Each participant is given an equal number of votes—three, four, or five. The votes are represented by colored stickers or checks on a flip chart or greaseboard where the brainstorming outputs are recorded. The participants can use their votes as they wish, spreading them around or consolidating them on a single idea. After everyone has been given a chance to record his or her preferences, the facilitator tallies the votes, and the idea with the most votes is chosen for implementation.

TRACKING PROJECTS TO COMPLETION

Before participants leave the review meeting, everyone should agree on the project(s) that will be pursued. Someone also should be designated as the project manager, responsible for planning the project, marshalling resources, and driving the effort through to completion. The project should also be documented in some way, to track it through the various stages to completion. A particularly good way to document improvement projects is through the corrective and preventive action system, familiar to all ISO 9001-registered organizations. Specifically, pure improvements work very well as preventive actions, a category of action that organizations often have trouble generating.

Many people find the notion of documenting improvement actions in the preventive action system very odd. However, there are good reasons for doing it. Here are just a few:

- Improvement actions really are preventive actions. By taking action to improve, the organization is preventing disaster, which is exactly what will happen if continual improvement of key measures isn't embraced. Improvement is the most proactive and strongest kind of prevention.
- Preventive (and corrective) action systems are designed as mini-project management systems. They're perfect for tracking actions through stages, reviewing progress to completion, and verifying effectiveness.
- Companies seem to have a very hard time documenting so-called preventive actions. Inputting pure improvement actions into this category will bolster the system and give it new relevance.

A combined corrective and preventive action form is shown in the appendix to chapter six, on page 95. Techniques for managing preventive and corrective actions systems are also shown.

ANALYSIS AND ACTION THROUGHOUT THE ORGANIZATION

This chapter has focused on analysis and action that takes place at the top of the organization. This is critical because it demonstrates top management's commitment and belief in key measures as a strategic tool. However, analysis and action can and should take place throughout the organization. In fact, the continual improvement system relies on the full involvement of everyone.

Processes should be established in every functional area for reviewing progress toward key measures. If the function has lower-level metrics that are directly linked to key measures, those metrics should be reviewed. Forums that are perfectly suited for reviewing metrics include departmental staff meetings, plant meetings, shift meetings, and morning coordination sessions. If possible, use existing performance reviews and only invent new meetings when absolutely necessary.

The same guidelines we already discussed also apply to reviewing metrics at lower levels of the organization:

- Converting raw data to graphics (e.g., bar charts, pie charts, Pareto diagrams) to facilitate interpretation
- Analyzing trends by the group
- Brainstorming improvement ideas aimed at achieving targets

■ Prioritizing improvement actions and ideas
■ Assigning project managers to the actions selected for implementation

The system of continual improvement comes to life once top management takes action to improve key measures, and everybody else gets an opportunity to do the same. Analysis and action must take place on the top-management level and throughout departments and processes for the system to be leveraged to its fullest.

DOS AND DON'TS OF ACTION AND ANALYSIS

As your organization begins to analyze progress against key measures and take improvement actions, the following issues should be considered:

✔ *Do document the process.* Write a documented procedure to guide analysis and action on key measures.

✔ *Do start at the top.* Get top management engaged and enthusiastic about taking action on key measures. When the rest of the organization sees that top management is serious about using key measures for action and decision making, everyone will want to be part of the process.

✔ *Do strive for diversity.* The wider the range of participants during the key measures review, the richer the analysis will be. A diverse range of participants will also help prevent groupthink.

✔ *Do brainstorm improvements.* Generate potential actions for improving key measures each time they're reviewed. Use tools such as the improvement needs assessment for prioritizing brainstorming outputs.

✔ *Do assign project managers.* All improvement actions that are selected for implementation should be assigned to a project manager. Track progress to completion by inputting actions into the preventive action system or other project management tools.

✗ *Don't invent new review meetings.* Use existing forums for reviewing key measures.

✗ *Don't present raw data for analysis.* Convert numbers to simple graphic tools to facilitate their interpretation.

✗ *Don't arbitrarily set targets.* Targets on key measures should only be set with an understanding of the variables underlying the measures. You might have to measure something for a number of weeks or months before you know enough to set targets.

✗ *Don't neglect any part of the organization for analysis and action.* At some level, everyone must be involved in the analysis and action of key measures for the organization to fully benefit from the system.

✗ *Don't separate ISO 9001 management reviews from the key measures review.* Put them together, and both systems will benefit enormously.

✗ *Don't neglect practical improvement ideas.* Many improvement ideas will have high practical benefit and low risk but seemingly little relevance to key measures. If the action improves any of your core business processes, then it has some link to key measures.

Chapter Four Appendix

BUSINESS REVIEW PROCEDURE

1. Purpose/scope

The purpose of this procedure is to guide the key measures review and related performance indicators at the organization's highest levels. The ultimate objective is to drive continual improvement on a strategic level, ensuring competitive advantage and long-term success. Business reviews also serve as ISO 9001:2000 management reviews.

2. Definitions

2.1. Key measures: The high-level metrics that indicate success against the organization's mission and strategy.

2.2. Business review council: The group of leaders responsible for reviewing organizational performance at the highest levels, and for proposing and managing actions aimed at improving organizational performance.

3. Frequency

3.1. Business review meetings take place at least once every two months, though the target frequency is once per month.

3.2. More frequent business review meetings will take place at management's discretion.

4. Participants

4.1. The business review council includes the president, chief operating officer, director of engineering, director of human resources, chief financial officer, vice president of technical services, vice president of sales, director of logistics, and the executive administrator. Other personnel can participate in the business review meeting on an as needed basis.

4.2. The following members of the business review council must be physically present for a business review meeting to be conducted (Proxies may not be sent in their place):

■ President

■ Chief financial officer

■ Director of engineering

4.3. At least four of the following individuals must be represented (either in person or through a proxy) for a business review meeting to be conducted:
- Chief operating officer
- Director of human resources
- Vice president of technical services
- Vice president of sales
- Director of logistics
- Executive administrator

5. Meeting preparation

5.1. At least one day prior to the business review meeting, the executive administrator will provide participants with data and/or charts illustrating progress toward key measures.

5.2. Participants in the business review meeting are expected to familiarize themselves with performance trends in advance of the meeting in order to facilitate business review proceedings.

6. Facilitation

6.1. Business review meetings are facilitated by the president or chief financial officer.

7. Business review inputs

7.1. The following issues are discussed and analyzed during the business review meeting. Discussion and analysis is led by the individual who provides the data. However, discussion of key measures is led by the chief financial officer.
- *Key measures:* provided in advance by the executive administrator
- *Results of audits (external and internal):* provided by the director of engineering
- *Customer feedback:* provided by vice president of sales
- *Process performance and product conformity:* provided by the director of engineering
- *Status of corrective and preventive actions:* provided by the chief operating officer
- *Follow-up actions from previous business review meetings:* provided by the president
- *Changes in the competitive, economic, and political environment that could affect the organization's success:* provided by the president

- *Recommendations for improvement:* solicited from the entire group (See section eight)
- *Adequacy of mission statement (reviewed at least once a year during one of the business review meetings):* provided by the president

8. Business review outputs

8.1. Business review meetings will provide four primary outputs. These will be in the form of actions or decisions related to each of the following:

- Improving key measures
- Effectiveness of company processes and management system
- Improving products and services
- Resource needs

8.2. Actions will be recorded and tracked through the corrective and preventive action system:

- Actions to address discrete failures or nonconformances will be recorded and tracked within the corrective action system.
- Actions to address potential failures or nonconformances, trends, and pure improvement ideas will be recorded and tracked within the preventive action system.
- In either case, actions will also be recorded in the business review meeting minutes.

8.3. The chief operating officer is responsible for ensuring that actions are entered into the corrective and/or preventive action system(s).

8.4. Decisions that don't result in actions will be recorded in business review meeting minutes only.

9. Records

9.1. The executive administrator is responsible for recording minutes of the business review.

9.2. Minutes and official records of the business review meeting will be stored and maintained in accordance with the records matrix (refer to document QA-9).

Figure 4.2: Improvement Needs Assessment

Date: ___/___/___ Location/Dept.: _____

Key Measure:

Proposed improvement actions:	Action linked to key measure(s)? 1 = No 3 = Yes	Action likely to result in cost reductions? 1 = No 3 = Yes	Positive effect on employee morale and/or motivation (1 = none or little, 2 = medium, 3 = high)

Action(s) selected for implementation: _____

_____

Reference corrective/preventive action(s) No.: _____

_____

				INA No. _____
Completed by: _____ _____ _____				

Importance to customer (1 = none or little, 2 = medium, 3= high)	Importance to internal operations (1 = none or little, 2 = medium, 3= high)	Degree of control over problem or opportunity (1 = none or little, 2 = medium, 3 = high)	Resources available for implementation (1 = none or few, 2 = medium or N/A, 3 = abundant)	Product of all columns (multiply them)

Additional justification (if applicable): _____

_____

Figure 4.3: Improvement Needs Assessment (completed example)

Date: ___/___/___ Location/Dept.: _____

Key Measure: Decrease employee turnover

Proposed improvement actions:	Action linked to key measure(s)? 1 = No 3 = Yes	Action likely to result in cost reductions? 1 = No 3 = Yes	Positive effect on employee morale and/or motivation (1 = none or little, 2 = medium, 3 = high)
1. Start providing free lunches to employees on Fridays	1	1	2
2. Design a training program on practical problem-solving techniques for all employees	3	1	3
3. Start doing exit interviews on employees at the time that they quit	3	1	1

Action(s) selected for implementation: _____

_____

Reference corrective/preventive action(s) No.: _____

_____

				INA No. _____
Completed by: _____ _____ _____				
Importance to customer (1 = none or little, 2 = medium, 3= high)	Importance to internal operations (1 = none or little, 2 = medium, 3= high)	Degree of control over problem or opportunity (1 = none or little, 2 = medium, 3 = high)	Resources available for implementation (1 = none or few, 2 = medium or N/A, 3 = abundant)	Product of all columns (multiply them)
1	1	2	1	4
3	3	3	1	243
1	2	2	2	24
Additional justification (if applicable): _____ _____				

Chapter Five

Process Orientation

F or most organizations, process orientation represents one of the biggest improvement opportunities available to them. It also requires a huge change in the way most organizations view and manage themselves. With process orientation, an organization defines itself as a system of integrated processes rather than a confederation of functional departments. There's nothing inherently wrong with managing by departments, but problems arise when they're managed semiautonomously. Each department manager attempts to maximize his or her results without considering how this affects other aspects of the production process. In addition, departmental divisions cause countless problems related to communication, coordination, and resources—all of which result in poor performance because the organization isn't structured to operate as effectively as possible.

Before we go further, let's consider what's meant by a process. Very simply, a process is an activity or bundle of activities that take inputs and transform them into products or outputs. This is an extremely broad definition, of course, and just about any activity could qualify as a process. For the purposes of this chapter, we'll concern ourselves with major business processes, those handful of primary transformation activities within an organization. Even the most complex organization probably has fewer than twenty major business processes. These work together in an integrated manner to carry out the organization's strategy and achieve its mission.

Anyone reading this would probably say, "Managing a business in terms of business processes makes perfect sense. Why would an organization manage itself any other way?" In fact, most organizations are divided into groups of functional activities—people doing similar activities grouped together, and all reporting to the same manager. Once this group finishes its work, the product is handed off to the next functional department and forgotten.

As an illustration, consider a widget manufacturer. The three key activities in widget manufacturing are stamping, grinding, and polishing. A traditional widget manufacturer divides these activities into individual departments, each with its own manager, staff, equipment, and supplies, as shown in Figure 5.1.

From one perspective, this organizational structure makes a lot of sense. The work is cleanly divided into discrete activities, with specialists doing their jobs and only their jobs. It's easy to measure the output of individual activities. Frederick Taylor and Henry Ford used this approach to achieve new levels of employee productivity and control at the beginning of the twentieth century. With cleanly divided departments, employees focus on their own work and little else.

Ironically, this benefit is also a big drawback to the departmental approach. People are so tightly focused that they don't really understand how their work fits into the organization's larger goals. The goal begins and ends with each department trying to excel individually, rather than the entire organization doing so. Each department measures its output and its efficiency, improving its performance on a micro level. This organizational structure works fairly well when an organization makes a few different products in large numbers, and it

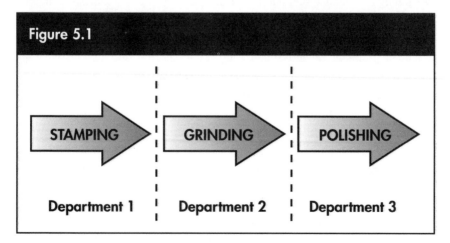

Figure 5.1

STAMPING   GRINDING   POLISHING

Department 1   **Department 2**   **Department 3**

sells everything it makes. The structure causes problems when the product list expands and mass customization is required. Of course, these days a wide product list and mass customization are more or less rules for both manufacturers and service providers.

The departmental approach's other drawback is that resources can't be easily shared across departments. Personnel are trained to do jobs in their departments only. They can't be redirected to activities in other departments because they don't know anything about them. Even if they could, what would be the advantage in the eyes of department managers? They're measured on the output of their own departments, not someone else's. As a result, the organization lacks the flexibility to apply people where they're needed on a moment's notice.

Personnel aren't the only resources that get snagged on departmental boundaries. Supplies and materials also don't flow easily across these divisions. Because supplies and materials are allocated to departments, there's little motivation to share these things when other departments need them. At the very least, delays occur as the details are worked out and managers find out how they can benefit from the situation. "What do you have that I can use?" is a question that's often heard in such situations. Again, everyone jockeys for position and tries to increase his or her own department's performance. After all, most departmental managers are compensated on their department's performance, so they can't be blamed for this behavior.

The last important resource that has trouble traveling across departmental boundaries is information. The departmental structure sets up a filter between information and the people who must receive it. Feedback on work conformance between one department and the next is delayed or blocked altogether. Many organizations forbid personnel to leave their departments and interact with people from other departments. Does this block information flow? Certainly. Even without such explicit prohibitions, the fact that departmental divisions exist poses an obstacle to personnel receiving feedback about their work farther down the line. This block reinforces the tendency for departments to think of themselves as little islands, operating independently of other activities.

Consider how the illustration in Figure 5.2 differs from the one we've been discussing.

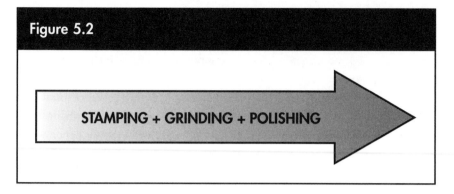

Figure 5.2

STAMPING + GRINDING + POLISHING

The functional activities of stamping, grinding, and polishing are recognized as part of the same process. No departmental boundaries exist between these activities. Personnel are cross-trained on different jobs so they can move from one activity to the next, based on the workload. Flexibility is built into the structure. Without departmental boundaries, all resources flow smoothly between activities, too. Information, supplies, and materials all go where they're needed, when they're needed. The entire process is managed by one person, whose compensation is based on the performance of the process rather than one aspect of it.

An organizational structure based on major processes makes perfect sense, but it's a radical departure for most enterprises. Managers usually have come of age in a world where companies consisted of functional departments, not integrated processes. Thinking about processes and how they function requires a different mindset than what's needed to run a functional department. The missing element is the link between one activity and the next. With functional departments, these links are taken for granted. If each department does its part, then the organization will succeed. Little consideration is given to the departmental links, although most problems occur there.

Process orientation highlights the links between activities because links simply are part of the process. They aren't disguised by departmental boundaries. Within a true process orientation it becomes immediately apparent if the links aren't effective. The connections between activities become smoother because the process's dynamic nature demands that they continually improve.

Process orientation's inherent clarity encourages organizations to use teams. Supervision is important when people must be pushed and directed, a situation that occurs when nobody really understands how the overall process works. In an organization that has adopted a process orientation, everybody can clearly see how the various activities fit together and support one another.

They see and understand the results of their efforts, and supervision becomes less necessary. Process orientation thus serves as a stepping-stone toward self-directed work teams and team problem solving.

In almost every way, process orientation is superior to traditional departmental structure. The following summarizes the attributes of a functional department vs. an integrated process.

A functional department encourages:

- Specialization
- Improvement efforts focused at the activity level
- Each activity to be fully staffed
- All personnel and equipment be used
- Little understanding of interdependencies between activities and processes
- Need for close supervision
- Localized communication
- Slow feedback from downstream activities
- Metrics focused on the activity
- Narrow accountability
- Little flexibility in the event of changes
- Competition for resources
- Inward-looking view
- Clear divisions between management and staff

An integrated process encourages:

- Broad competencies
- Improvement efforts focused at the process level
- Activities staffed only when needed
- Personnel and equipment used when demand requires them
- Heightened understanding of interdependencies between activities and processes
- Less need for supervision
- Global, free-flowing communications
- Fast feedback from downstream activities
- Metrics focused on the overall process
- Broad accountability
- Flexibility when changes occur
- Sharing of resources
- Outward-looking view
- Blurred divisions between management and staff

TYPICAL BUSINESS PROCESSES

Major business processes, which are supported by many subprocesses, sometimes coincide with traditional departmental boundaries but more often cut across them. People spend a lot of time figuring out where to draw the lines between major processes. It's worth vigorous discussion but not worth getting too hung up on. Each business process could easily be defined from a number of different angles. What's important is that the organization broadens its focus and attempts to embrace a structure other than just functional departments. That alone is a huge breakthrough.

Let's look at some examples of major business processes and their subprocesses.

Leadership
- Determining mission
- Developing strategy
- Selecting key measures
- Communicating mission, strategy, and key measures
- Ensuring that all processes are customer-focused
- Analyzing data
- Making rational decisions
- Recognizing personnel for their contributions
- Representing the organization in public life
- Acting ethically

Customer satisfaction process
- Conducting research into market needs and desires
- Communicating market needs and desires to other processes
- Developing marketing strategy
- Locating potential customers
- Providing product information
- Selling
- Performing sales follow-up
- Gauging customer perceptions
- Analyzing data on customer perceptions
- Communicating customer perceptions to the organization

Design process
- Understanding market needs and desires

- Converting needs and desires into design inputs
- Planning design activities
- Coordinating activities with all process leaders
- Developing product outputs that meet design inputs
- Reviewing design progress
- Verifying and validating design outputs
- Communicating design information to other processes
- Controlling design documents

Inbound process
- Communicating needs to suppliers
- Evaluating and selecting suppliers
- Purchasing supplies, services, and equipment (i.e., inbound products)
- Verifying the conformity of inbound products
- Ensuring payment of suppliers
- Providing feedback to suppliers about performance
- Moving inbound products to appropriate locations
- Storing inbound products as necessary
- Optimizing time, cost, and performance of inbound products

Product realization process (for manufacturing or service)
- Communicating supply, service, and equipment needs to inbound process
- Scheduling work
- Arranging resources
- Producing product through appropriate transformation activities
- Verifying product conformity
- Providing feedback to all activities within the process
- Packaging product as appropriate
- Applying all identifiers to product as appropriate
- Final product release

Outbound process
- Handling final product
- Scheduling transportation
- Storing product
- Ensuring preservation
- Picking orders

☐ Loading trucks
■ Coordinating delivery with customers

Personnel management process

☐ Determining personnel competency needs in cooperation with process leaders
☐ Recruiting appropriate personnel
■ Assigning personnel to processes
☐ Determining appropriate compensation and benefits packages
☐ Developing policies that result in employee retention
■ Facilitating organizational communications
■ Mediating conflict
☐ Ensuring legal compliance
☐ Administering programs to build competencies (e.g., training)

Maintenance process

☐ Providing maintainability requirements to inbound process owners
☐ Determining and implementing preventive and predictive maintenance
■ Scheduling maintenance in the most efficient manner possible
☐ Reacting to breakdown scenarios
☐ Performing preventive and predictive maintenance
☐ Optimizing infrastructure cost, timing, and effectiveness

Improvement process

■ Guiding development of procedures
☐ Managing internal audits
■ Administering corrective and preventive actions
☐ Reporting to leadership and other processes on the results of improvement efforts
■ Facilitating the problem-solving methods and tools
■ Troubleshooting with customers
☐ Assisting in the improvement of suppliers
■ Guiding the use of statistical techniques
■ Identifying and removing nonvalue-added activities
■ Soliciting improvement ideas from personnel
☐ Ensuring the recognition of personnel
■ Supervising the investigation into product and service failures

Drawing the lines between business processes is something of a balancing act. An organization usually benefits when a business process cuts as broadly as possible through the organization, though a process that cuts too broadly is difficult to control. Defining the end of one business process and the start of another is a matter of subjective judgment and what can only be called process wisdom. However, a couple of guidelines can assist in defining the processes:

- A business process includes subprocesses that add value to a product in the same general manner. The subprocesses don't necessarily need to be similar to one another, but they must work toward a common destination.
- A business process includes subprocesses that have the same general objective, such as acquiring the best supplies and materials at a competitive cost, or transforming the product in the most efficient manner possible.

Avoid the temptation to define processes along the same boundaries as functional departments. The whole point of process orientation is to combat the narrow, myopic perspectives that functional departments often encourage. Simply calling a functional department by a different name does nothing for the organization.

BEGINNING THE JOURNEY

In a perfect world, restructuring an organization along business processes lines would be a simple action. However, nobody resides in a perfect world. Organizational changes of this magnitude carry with them significant implications, and only top managers can carry them out successfully. Even then, the changes sometimes still fall short.

Evolving toward process orientation is the best solution. Many practical actions can be implemented that will gradually shift your organization toward a process orientation, and these can be implemented by anyone with organizational respect and clout. The actions' cumulative effect is great, but taken incrementally and slowly they're much easier to implement.

1. Determine the business processes that exist within the organization.
2. Compare the boundaries of business processes with existing functional departments to determine where conflicts exist.
3. Develop process flow diagrams that span departmental boundaries and depict business processes in their entirety.
4. Cross-train personnel who work within the same business process.

5. Assign cross-trained personnel to new activities to build flexibility and heighten awareness of the integrated process.

6. Examine incentives and objectives across functional departments. Do they encourage functional departments to improve at the expense of business processes? Remove all incentives and objectives that suboptimize the organization's overall performance.

7. Establish opportunities for personnel to interact within and across business processes. Encourage frequent dialogue. Some of the best improvement ideas come serendipitously through informal discussion.

8. Encourage personnel to communicate ideas for improvement. Focus personnel on the improvement of business processes, not just the improvement of narrow tasks and activities.

9. Eliminate activities that don't add value or contribute to the effective functioning of the business process.

10. As personnel and managers become accustomed to thinking in terms of business processes instead of functional activities, begin reshaping the organization's formal structure toward a process orientation.

Process orientation is a relatively abstract concept. It's helpful to see what other organizations have done to change their structures from departmental to process orientation. It's worth noting that the transformation is a process in itself, one that might require many small, incremental steps.

BRIGGS AND STRATTON POWER PRODUCTS

Jim Hineline, director of quality at Briggs and Stratton Power Products in Jefferson, Wisconsin, provides an example of how his facility made organizational changes to better reflect a process orientation. "For many years, our receiving activities were separate from the incoming inspection activities," he explains. "Receiving department personnel would schedule trucks at docks, unload trailers, stage materials, and request that the quality control (QC) department perform its incoming inspection. Sometime later, the QC department would perform incoming inspection. After the inspection, the material would be moved back to receiving for further staging or storage." Instead of a smooth process flow, the receiving process had been divided between two departments, causing frequent delays, communication breakdowns, and process inefficiencies. The need to change was apparent.

"We merged the incoming inspection activities into the regular duties of warehouse personnel," Hineline says. "Instead of handoffs between departments, all the receiving activities were conducted as an integrated process. The changes increased communications with the production process, shortened turnaround time, and generated more process ownership among personnel." Efficiency soared and costs dropped dramatically. Efficiency was improved so much, in fact, that five personnel were transferred to other parts of the facility because they were no longer necessary within the receiving process. "Of course, we found other places for these folks," he notes. "Firing people tends to sour everyone on continual improvement."

Despite the fact that Briggs and Stratton had made great strides in reducing incoming inspections, it was still an activity that took place numerous times throughout the week. Integrating the split activities of receiving and incoming inspection into a single process was a win-win proposition for everyone involved.

T&D REMARKETED SERVICES

T&D Remarketed Services in Alpharetta, Georgia, refurbishes Heidelberg printing presses. The company's process manager, Terry Waldrop, explained that process thinking is just a way of life at T&D. "Everything we do is structured by process," he says. "We have roughly twelve distinct production processes that are applied to printing presses. Nobody thinks in terms of functions or hierarchy, just processes: prep, cleaning, preassembly test, assembly, postassembly test, etc. We don't even have departments in the traditional sense." Waldrop explains that most employees don't even have job titles because they might be employed anywhere within the range of processes.

The work at T&D is controlled by a series of process checklists that are constantly revised and improved. A checklist might be revised a number of times during the course of the quarter as people working within the process receive feedback and find ways to improve their methods. The checklists are simple and easy to revise, and employees take ownership of their content. "They helped write them, and they're always in the process of improving them," Waldrop observes. "So why shouldn't they feel ownership? My job as process manager is to help everyone take more ownership over their processes."

Process orientation at T&D also has streamlined feedback. In fact, feedback is immediate because no departmental boundaries impede it. When problems pop up, personnel all over the production area will contribute to its solution. "It sounds almost anarchistic," says Waldrop, "but it's very tightly controlled by the employees themselves."

INTERFACE FLOORING

Interface Flooring in LaGrange, Georgia, is one of the world's foremost manufacturers of commercial carpet tile. They're also on the cutting edge of continual improvement and environmental protection. Billy Ingram, director of manufacturing services, relates one of their big successes with process orientation. "Our process of making tufted carpet had always included the departments of backwinding, beaming, tufting, and coating," he explains. "These departments had been in place so long, nobody even questioned them." However, problems occurred when the market began demanding a broader range of styles and smaller production runs. "The functions we had in place didn't enable us to respond quickly," he recalls. "Something had to change."

What changed was the company's view of itself. "We always thought of ourselves as a grouping of departments, all providing a little piece of a puzzle," says Ingram. "With that outlook, there was no way we were going to shorten our lead times and provide a wide range of styles." So instead, Ingram began to view the manufacturing activities as an integrated process. "Thinking of ourselves in a broader fashion, we were able to evaluate the value of each of the activities that contributed to the business process of making carpet," he adds. "The more we looked, the more we began to see that not all activities were necessary to achieve the end result."

It became clear that the backwinding and beaming activities could be consolidated. "We discovered that we could achieve the results of these activities without actually having them," he says. "All that time, effort, and expense could be avoided simply by reorienting our process." In the end, the beaming function was completely eliminated and the backwinding function reduced. The result was an integrated process that was nimble enough to produce short runs of many different styles at significantly reduced costs.

(Thanks also to Joey Milford for his contributions to this piece.)

DOS AND DON'TS OF PROCESS ORIENTATION

Embracing a process orientation is a complex, long-term journey but one that will produce significant organizational improvements. As you maneuver your organization down this path keep these dos and don'ts on your radar screen:

✔ *Do determine major business processes.* Study the logical streams of subprocesses and figure out where the true business processes lie.

✔ *Do look for process interrupts.* Seek out places where a process's smooth operation is interrupted by departmental boundaries. Activities surrounding these interrupts might be candidates for consolidation.

✔ *Do depict processes graphically.* People will grasp the concept of business processes if they're able to see how the pieces fit together.

✔ *Do give employees a degree of ownership.* Involve them in the documenting of the process, problem solving, and generating improvement ideas.

✘ *Don't create a process revolution.* The entire organization needn't adopt a process orientation simultaneously. Incremental changes will be easier to implement and more effective in the long run.

✘ *Don't be afraid of challenging entrenched practices.* Many activities are in place for no other reason than the fact they've always been there. If an activity or function adds no value to the business process, it's a candidate for removal.

✘ *Don't make victims.* Don't let the journey of becoming process oriented turn into an exercise in laying off people. If activities are eliminated or consolidated, find places for the people in other parts of the operation whenever possible.

Chapter Six

Effective Problem Solving

In This Chapter
- Problem-Solving Fundamentals
- Problem-Solving Tools
- Corrective and Preventive Action Procedure
- Root Cause Analysis Procedure

So far this book has focused on proactive means of driving continual improvement: understanding mission and strategy, defining key measures, analyzing data, and moving toward a process orientation. These techniques keep everybody's eyes fixed on continual improvement as a perennial organizational theme. However, every now and then things don't go as planned. Problems come up, equipment breaks down, people make mistakes, customers complain. This is when the organization shifts into a reactive mode. How effectively the organization reacts will determine if continual improvement happens or not. This is why it's critical that the organization embraces systematic methods for problem solving.

Theoretically, using problem solving to drive continual improvement is simple. A problem or potential problem comes up, its root cause is identified, and action is taken to eliminate it. If the organization progressively seeks out and eliminates problems in this way, then continual improvement results. It's that simple.

What's not so simple is learning how to make this happen in a practical sense. Talking about problem solving as a cornerstone of continual improvement is easy, but making it happen in a systematic and effective manner is much harder. During the years that I've been involved in problem solving in diverse organizations, I've recognized seven fundamentals that were almost always present when problems were solved in a lasting and effective way.

FIRST FUNDAMENTAL: USE A STRUCTURED PROBLEM-SOLVING METHOD

A problem-solving method is simply a step-by-step road map for solving problems. It tells what to do first, second, third, and so forth. The notion of using a structured problem-solving method sounds almost infantile to most people these days, but the fact is that most organizations still use a completely ad hoc method for solving problems.

The reasons for using a formal problem-solving method are convincing, including:

■ *To prevent problem solvers from jumping to conclusions.* It's always tempting to propose solutions before the problem is properly defined and the root cause identified. A structured problem-solving method prevents the process from short-circuiting and enforces the critical, preliminary steps of understanding the problem and its variables.

■ *To enforce root cause analysis.* Inability (or unwillingness) to identify root cause is probably the single largest obstacle to problem solving. When one of the explicit steps within the structured problem-solving method is identifying root cause, it's much harder to ignore.

■ *To demystify the problem-solving process.* Each step of the problem-solving method is understood and agreed upon by the users. This commonality gives all process participants equal opportunity to contribute and drives a democratic form of problem solving.

■ *To provide guidance on the use of analytical tools.* The sheer number of analytical tools available to problem solvers is mind boggling, and it's not always clear when the use of a certain tool is appropriate. A structured problem-solving method offers guidelines on when and how to use the proper tools.

Innumerable problem-solving methods exist. Some are copyrighted, some are public domain, some are intricate, and others are quite simple. Typically they range in complexity from four to eight steps. However, all problem-solving methods share the same basic themes. It's not really important which method you use, but make sure to pick one and use it. You can even make up your own.

For those who aren't feeling particularly creative, you're welcome to adopt the one that follows. It's a hybrid, basic problem-solving method that accommodates my own sensibilities and provides for all the necessary activities.

1. *Decide on what problem to pursue.* For some reason, this step is left out of many problem-solving methods. Maybe people assume that the problems worth tackling are obvious. This is hardly ever the case. Countless opportunities for improvement (along with finite resources) are the norm for most organizations. Effective organizations prioritize issues and dedicate resources accordingly. Appropriate tools include brainstorming, Pareto charts, run charts, pie charts, flow diagrams, and multivoting.

2. *Define the problem.* In the clearest and most succinct terms possible, state what exactly is the problem. Provide the details of who, what, where, and when. A problem definition along the lines of, "The customer complains that the parts won't run right," is almost worthless. Be specific. Remember that problem definition provides the raw material for successful root cause identification. Appropriate tools include brainstorming, Pareto charts, check sheets, and histograms.

3. *Determine root cause.* Identifying root cause proceeds directly from problem definition. The typical obstacle at this step is confusing the symptom with the root cause. Often this manifests itself by the so-called root cause being nothing more than a restatement of the problem in slightly different words. Problem solvers should receive training in how to distinguish symptoms from root causes before they're ever asked to solve their first problem, but this rarely happens. Appropriate tools include interviewing, brainstorming, cause-and-effect diagrams, and multivoting.

4. *Generate possible solutions and choose the most likely one.* This step works well in a team setting, where it's possible to generate a large number of alternative solutions. The trick is to cast a wide net, then narrow the field to those solutions that satisfy the following criteria:

   ■ They have a strong chance of being successfully implemented.
   ■ They will be accepted by all relevant stakeholders.
   ■ They address the root cause identified in the previous step.

   Finally, a solution is agreed upon, either by group consensus or through executive decree. Appropriate tools include brainstorming, Pareto diagrams, and multivoting.

5. *Plan and execute the solution.* Even the best solution is doomed to failure if its implementation isn't carefully planned and executed. This typically consists of two distinct phases: selling the solution to key stakeholders and methodical project planning to ensure the solution is executed correctly. It's also helpful to notify the customers who will be affected by the

solution and let them know what's happening. This reinforces the idea that the organization is dedicated to customer satisfaction and problem resolution. Appropriate tools include project planning, selling skills, and pilot runs.

6. *Verify effectiveness.* After you think you've implemented your solution, somebody must verify that it's effective. The more objective this determination, the better. It isn't absolutely necessary that people outside of the problem-solving team verify effectiveness, but it might avoid bias. A technical understanding of the action's underlying issues will also help. If you're dealing with a document control problem, the technical aspects probably will be relatively minor. If you're talking about retrofitting an extruder screw to improve the plasticity of a synthetic polymer, the technical aspects become more complicated. Use common sense when assigning someone to verify an action's effectiveness.

What exactly should verification seek to prove? At a minimum, three types of evidence should be sought:

■ The action taken relates to the identified root cause
■ The action was actually implemented
■ The action was effective in preventing the problem from recurring (clearly the most important detail to verify)

Typically, this type of evidence might take some time to compile, requiring that actions remain open longer than expected. It's better that actions remain open and ultimately lead to a true solution to the problem, rather than closing actions prematurely to achieve clean records.

Customers, both internal and external, are particularly good at shedding light on a solution's effectiveness. If the customer doesn't perceive an improvement, then there isn't any; perception is everything. Appropriate tools include auditing, interviewing, control charts, and process capability studies.

7. *Document the improvement.* Once the action's effectiveness has been confirmed, the improvement must be documented. This could involve developing completely new documentation or revising existing documentation. The imperative of documentation is clear: It solidifies improvements so that problems don't recur. Without documentation, it's debatable whether an improvement was even made because it's likely to be temporary. Documentation puts the capstone on the problem-solving process.

The manner in which improvements are documented is as important as the improvements themselves. Documentation that's inconvenient or confusing will be ignored, and the improvements included therein will be useless. This means that the problem-solving process fails at the final step, after much time and energy has been expended.

Keep these points in mind when documenting any process, especially improvements:

■ *Determine from the user the most convenient type and location of documentation.* What will work best—a traditional procedure, a specification sheet, a flowchart, a drawing, a photograph? Consider the documentation user as your customer, and strive to accommodate his or her wishes whenever practical.

■ *Record documentation in the most simple and graphic form possible.* Text-based procedures should be used only when there's no more efficient way to present the information.

■ *Place documentation at the point of use.* Develop creative methods for making the information available where people can refer to it. Instructions located in supervisors' offices or training rooms are essentially useless.

■ *Use electronic documentation whenever possible.* It requires a certain level of infrastructure and expertise to implement, but it facilitates quick updating, review, approval, and delivery of documentation.

■ *Remove bureaucracy from the document control process.* Maintain control, but simplify and streamline the process. The more approvals a document requires, the more burdensome the document control process will be. The same goes for rigid protocols related to document style, formatting, and content.

Documentation that's convenient, easy to use, and available where it's needed is the best way to complete the problem-solving cycle, and continually improving documentation will help drive continual improvement.

Not every problem can be solved effectively through a structured problem-solving method, but most can. Select a method and commit to using it at all levels of your organization. Then train everyone on the method. Make it an institution. A tool of this sort becomes stronger with regular use, so exploit every opportunity for applying it.

Each of the remaining fundamentals could be considered components of the problem-solving method we just explored, but they're still important enough to discuss separately.

SECOND FUNDAMENTAL: ASSIGN OWNERSHIP FOR THE PROBLEM

Even if your organization uses a team approach to problem solving, every problem should be assigned to a specific individual. Confirm that the individual accepts ownership. The owner is simply the project manager for solving the problem. Make sure that the individual understands that being assigned this role in no way accuses him or her or assigns blame. In fact, it's a vote of confidence for the person's ability as a leader and project manager.

Each problem's project manager is responsible for recruiting the team members (if a team approach is appropriate), acquiring resources, leading the investigation into root cause, facilitating the selection of possible actions, and ensuring that the action is implemented. Having one person responsible for the overall process creates a level of commitment that's difficult to achieve otherwise. As W. Edwards Deming so famously said, "Shared responsibility means that nobody is responsible."

It's pleasant to think that problems assigned to committees will get solved. Sometimes this might even happen. However, the vast majority of successful problem-solving projects are led by individuals accountable for the endeavor's success. Ownership can do remarkable things. Don't neglect it.

THIRD FUNDAMENTAL: INVOLVE PEOPLE FAMILIAR WITH THE PROBLEM

The people most familiar with the variables surrounding the problem should be involved in the problem-solving process. These people often aren't managers and supervisors but rather those who take the orders, write the software, operate the machines, drive the forklifts, and perform the repairs. The organization's culture must allow for all personnel's active contribution, regardless of their level within the organization.

One of the project manager's most important tasks will be to select the right people for the problem-solving team. After selection, participants should be told why they've been included (e.g., because of their technical expertise, familiarity with the processes in question, or experience with the product line). It's important that individuals are motivated and enthusiastic about being involved.

Including a diverse selection of personnel in the problem-solving process also has profound organizational benefits. More people will benefit from the learning opportunity that results from the experience. The more people who take part in problem solving, the better the organization becomes at addressing problems effectively. Gradually, using a structured problem-solving method will become second nature, and a deep belief in continual improvement starts to take hold.

FOURTH FUNDAMENTAL: APPLY PROJECT MANAGEMENT TECHNIQUES

Project management is a basic concept. In fact, it's nothing more than assigning responsibilities, time frames, milestones, and reviews, as well as tracking progress to completion. These are all simple concepts, yet often neglected. Following through on an initiative of any complexity without project management is strictly a matter of luck, something that wise people won't count on in a pinch.

The corrective and preventive action system naturally embodies the basics of project management. If your corrective and preventive action system is user-friendly and streamlined, then it's a perfectly suitable tool for problem solving. If it's not user-friendly and streamlined, then it should be redesigned, quickly. Complexity isn't a strength of a corrective and preventive action system. Benchmark systems from other organizations, and don't be shy about borrowing best practices where you find them.

Consider the specific attributes of your corrective and preventive action system. If you use a paper-based system, the corrective action/preventive action request form should fit onto a single, one-sided piece of paper if possible. The longer and more complicated the form, the less receptive personnel will be to using it. The number of approval signatures should also be considered. Do you really need more than one or two signatures? Each signature adds days to the processing and contributes little or nothing to the effectiveness of the actions taken.

An electronic system is a viable option for many organizations. An e-mail system can be used to transmit corrective and preventive actions, even if the process consists of nothing more than attaching a file to an e-mail message. This also makes the system more usable for people outside the organization, such as suppliers and subcontractors. The simple act of transmitting corrective or preventive actions as e-mail attachments will save days in processing time.

A simple and effective corrective and preventive action form, along with the procedure for using it, are included in this chapter's appendix, on pages 95 and 92.

FIFTH FUNDAMENTAL: AGGRESSIVELY PURSUE ROOT CAUSE

One of the explicit steps of any problem-solving method is identifying root cause. However, just because it's an explicit step doesn't mean it's always successfully completed. Identifying the root cause must be enforced. The first line of enforcement is the project manager, who should ensure that the root cause has been identified. This isn't easy. It usually takes some serious investigation and intellectual tenacity. A root cause is rarely the first thing that comes to mind. Consider these supposed root causes:

■ *Employee error.* It's possible that employee error could have been a cause of the problem, but was it the *root* cause? Why exactly did the employee make the error? Why is the task prone to error? Clearly, employee error probably isn't the root cause, and any action directed at this cause won't make the problem go away.

■ *Failure to follow procedure.* Why didn't the employee follow procedure? Did he or she know the procedure existed? Were there other forces at play, possibly incentives that discourage adhering to the procedure? The corrective action for failing to follow procedure is usually a variation on, "employee was reprimanded." Do people really believe reprimands drive continual improvement? Not in any kind of organization I'd want to be a part of.

■ *Sloppy work.* This is another root cause that only skims the top of the issue. What exactly caused the sloppy work? A very small subset of employees might be naturally sloppy and require special attention. In most cases, however, sloppy work is a symptom of some other variable acting on the process.

The examples above illustrate the elusive nature of root cause. When you think you've identified it, ask "why" one more time. You might be surprised to find that a deeper reason lurks below the alleged root cause.

Let's take each of the superficial causes listed above and see if we can uncover the true root cause by continuing to ask why.

Scenario one

Superficial cause: Employee error

Why did the employee make the error? Because he used the wrong specification.

Why did the employee use the wrong specification? Because that's what he'd been given.

Why had the employee been given the wrong specification? Because the specification had been changed by the customer, and no procedures exist for correctly communicating a changed specification once the order has been released to the floor. *This is the real root cause.*

Corrective action: Develop procedures for communicating changed specifications. This action is preferable to training the employee, which would probably have been the solution suggested for the superficial cause. Training would accomplish nothing because the problem wasn't the employee but a flaw in the system.

Scenario two

Superficial cause: Failure to follow procedure

Why did the employee fail to follow procedure? Because a warehouse operator (the employee's internal customer) asked for some help, and this caused the employee to leave his operation.

Why did the warehouse operator ask for help? Because the palletizer had malfunctioned and there was no one else to help him.

Why did the palletizer malfunction? Because it ran out of hydraulic fluid.

Why did it run out of hydraulic fluid? Because checking for hydraulic fluid was not on the weekly preventive maintenance checklist. *This is the real root cause.*

Corrective action: Revise the weekly preventive maintenance checklist to include a check for hydraulic fluid. Again, this corrective action is quite different from the likely action—i.e., reprimand employee—that the superficial cause might have warranted.

Scenario three

Superficial cause: Sloppy work

Why was sloppy work performed? Because the employee didn't know any better.

Why didn't the employee know any better? Because training had never been carried out.

Why hadn't training been carried out? Because it had never been scheduled by the supervisor.

Why hadn't training been scheduled by the supervisor? Because the supervisor didn't believe that training was a good use of this employee's time. *This is the real root cause.*

Corrective action: Ensure that the supervisor understands the value of training. Give him or her some real-life examples, including the example from his or her own process. Make certain that training for the employee is scheduled and carried out. In this case, as with the previous two, the corrective action directed at the real root cause is drastically different than what would have been applied to the superficial cause.

In each of these scenarios, the real root cause was determined by continuing to ask why. There's no magic number of whys to ask. The root cause is generally the answer to the why that comes right before issues that the organization has no power to affect. If the whys have drilled down to something that's categorically impossible to take action on, go up one level, and you'll probably have the actionable root cause.

The root cause worksheet included in this chapter's appendix, on page 96, will help reinforce the exploration into the whys of a problem.

SIXTH FUNDAMENTAL: COMMUNICATE AND CONGRATULATE

Communication drives the success of problem solving at every stage. People crave information about how problems are addressed and solved. This information creates a feeling of security and confidence and builds an overall culture of continual improvement.

Make problem solving the subject of frequent communication within your organization. If a customer complaint gets addressed in an effective manner, tell the tale in the company newsletter. If a group of employees succeed in reducing the error rate, send everyone an e-mail trumpeting the achievement. If the quality assurance department assists a supplier in improving the consistency of its output, get the local newspaper to cover the story. Get the word out any time your organization succeeds in solving or preventing problems. The more employees hear about successes, the more they'll want to be involved. The more employees get involved, the more successful your company will be.

Dignified public recognition, of course, is a form of communication, and it offers an astronomical return on investment. The message is, "The company appreciates your team's fine efforts. We sincerely hope others will follow your example." Who wouldn't want to follow their example and be recognized, too? Congratulations should be dignified, public, and carried out by top management.

SEVENTH FUNDAMENTAL: START WITH SIMPLE TOOLS, BUT USE THEM WELL

In many of life's tasks, the simplest tools are the best. That axiom holds true in problem solving. Countless problem-solving tools exist, but the tools that are applied time and time again with a high degree of success are usually the simplest ones.

But just because something is simple doesn't mean it can be applied in a slipshod manner. Even the use of simple tools must be carefully planned and executed. Training is essential on their practical application, including concrete examples of how they work. The payoff is that once people understand how to use the tools, they immediately put them to use. The experience curve on these tools isn't very steep.

Let's take a look at a range of simple tools and how they might be applied.

Interviewing

This technique is rarely considered a problem-solving tool. Nevertheless, it's one of the most valuable when used at the beginning and end of the problem-solving process. Interviewing uncovers the details of the situation, which leads to a clear problem definition. Most people try to solve problems before they can even state its nature; this is a sure formula for failure. At the end of the problem-solving process, interviewing helps to determine whether corrective actions have been effective.

The term "interviewing" conjures notions of a formal, face-to-face meeting. This is a very narrow view of the activity. Interviewing can take place over the phone or via e-mail, and it certainly doesn't have to be formal. As long as an opportunity is made for dynamic interaction that gathers information, then interviewing is what you're doing.

What are the characteristics of effective interviewing? They're simple, but often overlooked:

■ *Don't use the term "interview."* When most people hear interview, they immediately become uneasy. The more uneasy someone is, the less able he or she is to provide useful information.

■ *Clearly state the purpose.* If you're trying to gather information about a product problem, simply state this purpose at the onset of the conversation. Don't be mysterious.

■ *Put the person at ease.* Make sure that the person knows the information he or she is providing will be used to improve something, not to get anyone in trouble.

■ *Get specifics.* Drill down to the core issues. As an interviewer, your primary role is to guide the person you're speaking with into providing the most accurate and detailed information possible. To elicit useful information you have to explore the issue from a number of angles (e.g., time of day, environmental conditions, and people involved.)

■ *Take notes.* Don't rely on your memory during an interview. Record all the details of the interview and don't be afraid of sharing these with the person with whom you're talking.

Brainstorming

As described in chapter four, this is a tool for generating wide ranging and numerous ideas. It leverages people's natural creativity in a group setting. Brainstorming is an excellent tool for the early stages of problem solving. People often have highly divergent opinions regarding root cause, and these opinions make for rich brainstorming input. Brainstorming can also be used to generate possible solutions after the root cause has been identified. The rules of brainstorming are quite simple:

■ *Select a facilitator.* This is the person who will enforce the rules of brainstorming and record the results.

■ *Solicit inputs from each person in turn.* The facilitator will record each input. The setting should be informal and relaxed.

■ *Refrain from criticizing or commenting on the inputs.* The more unconventional the input, the better. It could spark innovative thinking in others.

■ *Generate ideas until the group has exhausted all possible inputs.*

Cause-and-effect diagrams

Also known as fishbone diagrams, these tools organize causes in a graphic manner so their relationships can be more readily understood. The effect or problem is represented on the diagram as the fish's horizontal "spine." The cause categories branch off the spine in a series of "bones." The most typical bones shown on a cause-and-effect diagram are method, material, personnel, machines, and environment. However, virtually any categories could be represented.

These graphic tools are especially useful when determining root cause. In fact, a brainstorming session's output makes the perfect input for a cause-and-effect diagram. Each of the brainstormed causes is affixed to the appropriate bone that represents its category. The placement and magnitude of ideas on each bone of the diagram can reveal interesting relationships. For example, it might highlight that most possible causes fall into the machine category. The issue of machines could warrant deeper investigation. Cause-and-effect diagrams can also be used during brainstorming sessions to facilitate the input of ideas from all possible categories. Of course, participants in the brainstorming session aren't forced to make inputs that fall into certain categories, but the mere presence of the diagram can trigger thinking in interesting directions.

The power of cause-and-effect diagrams is simply the graphic representation of possible causes in an organized manner. Will such a diagram automatically reveal a problem's root cause? Probably not, but it will help problem solvers organize their ideas and sharpen their thinking. These two basic activities often lead to discovering the root cause. A sample cause-and-effect diagram is shown in Figure 6.1. This particular example seems to indicate that material issues might represent the largest contribution to late orders.

Figure 6.1: Cause-and-Effect Diagram

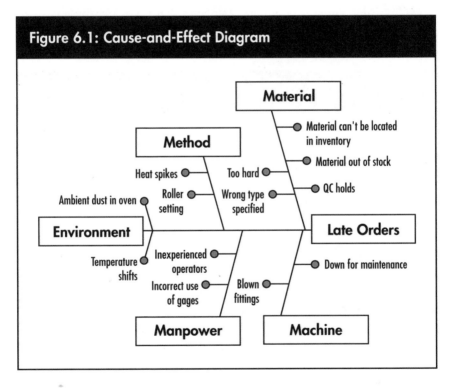

Pareto diagrams

Pareto diagrams are based on the late nineteenth and early twentieth century research of Italian economist Vilfredo Pareto. One of his observations can be paraphrased by saying that 80 percent of a society's wealth can be attributed to 20 percent of the population. This eighty-twenty rule or "Pareto

Principle" applies to many other phenomena. Consider the following distributions: 80 percent of all sales can be attributed to 20 percent of the salespeople; 80 percent of all complaints can be attributed to 20 percent of the defects; 80 percent of all warranty claims can be attributed to 20 percent of the products. Of course, percentages aren't exact, and the eighty-twenty ratio is only a ballpark estimate. The Pareto Principle is simply a way of attributing the majority of effects to a minority of causes.

In essence, a Pareto diagram is a bar graph constructed so that the leading contributor is shown first, the second largest contributor shown next, the third largest contributor is shown after that, and so on. This stair step, graphic approach makes it very easy to interpret data that might otherwise escape comprehension. Usually there's no doubt about the leading opportunity when data are converted to this type of format. In Figure 6.2 below, it's obvious that poor adhesion and paint smears are the two largest causes of problems, thus representing the most obvious targets for corrective actions.

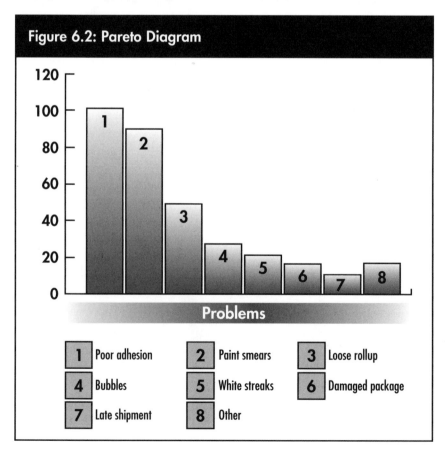

Figure 6.2: Pareto Diagram

Occasionally the first attempt at creating a Pareto diagram provides inconclusive results. Data might need to be rearranged into different categories to uncover the big opportunities. Look for slightly different ways to present the data (i.e., different categories), then reconstruct the diagram. The only caveat is that the categories must be logical.

Run charts

This tool converts raw data produced in time sequence into a chart that quickly reveals changes in level. The data can represent anything: temperature, defects, pressure, production output, or calls made. The time scale can be months, weeks, days, hours, or any other interval that's logically matched to the process being charted. A run chart's strength is in its simplicity and interpretation. Even a child can create and maintain a run chart, and anybody can detect changes in the data when they're depicted in this graphic manner.

Their one significant weakness is that they reveal nothing about the statistical significance of movements in the data. In other words, is that scary blip just normal variation in the process, or is it something to get excited about? A run chart won't tell you. Only a control chart with statistically derived control limits will communicate the nature of the variation.

When designing the X axis of the run chart, consider the data's historical movement. If they've typically fallen between eighty and one hundred, for instance, then a scale that encompasses a slightly larger interval (say, sixty to 120) should capture all possible data and still highlight changes in level. Also keep in mind that a run chart's simplicity is perfectly suited to being done by hand in real time. There's no need for fancy computer graphics. Just make sure the scales are clearly marked, and the users understand what they're supposed to do with them. In Figure 6.3, the number of defects per hour are plotted.

Flowcharts

These are among the most overlooked improvement tools. A flowchart is nothing more than graphic representation of a process. The most typical style flows from top to bottom in a linear manner, following a process through all the necessary tasks and decisions. A flowchart's power is twofold:

■ *It's extremely easy to understand and follow.* A process's actions and decisions all are obvious when depicted in a flowchart's graphic style. Procedures written in a traditional text format—e.g., bulleted paragraphs— are not as user-friendly. Besides providing clear guidance on the task activity level, flowcharts give a quick snapshot of the entire process from start to

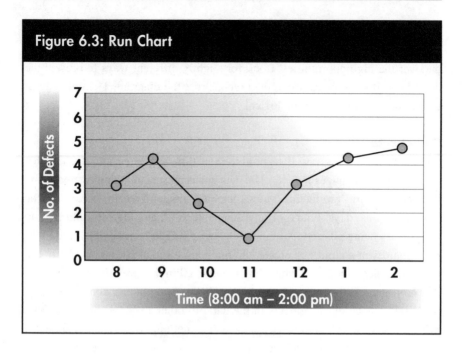

Figure 6.3: Run Chart

finish, and this big picture is very helpful for communicating exactly what the process is supposed to achieve.

■ *Inefficiencies in the process become quickly apparent.* Because the flow-chart depicts a process graphically, it's impossible to bury activities in the sort of descriptive text that sometimes inhabits traditional procedures. The activity steps that don't make sense often are revealed in stark relief. Needless movement and storage steps, misplaced verifications, and activities that don't add value to the process all become apparent in a flowchart.

Each task in the process is represented by a geometrically shaped box, within which the task is briefly described. The most common shape for a task box is a rectangle, though people often devise rules for the correct shape of special tasks such as movement, storage, or data input. Tasks are linked to one another via a line with an arrow. No task box has more than one arrow flowing out of it. The only exception is the case of a decision box—usually depicted as a diamond—and this will have two arrows flowing from it, one for "yes" and one for "no." These kinds of responses require that the decision be framed as a question, of course, but other responses could also be attached to the decision diamond. The terminal points on flowcharts often are depicted as ovals or circles.

It's actually easier to construct a flowchart than it is to write a procedure. The brevity required by the flowchart is a relief to most writers, who would prefer to use as few words as possible, anyway. Here are some points to keep in mind while constructing a flow diagram:

■ *Don't overwhelm the boxes with text.* Fit only a few words into each box.

■ *Keep the diagram simple.* Avoid lines that cross one another; this creates confusion in the task flow.

■ *Each task box should have only one arrow leaving it.* However, a decision box can have two or more arrows coming out of it, depending on the nature of the decision criteria presented in the box.

■ *Test your flowchart's logic by asking someone to follow the process by using the flowchart.*

A simplified example of a flowchart is shown in Figure 6.4

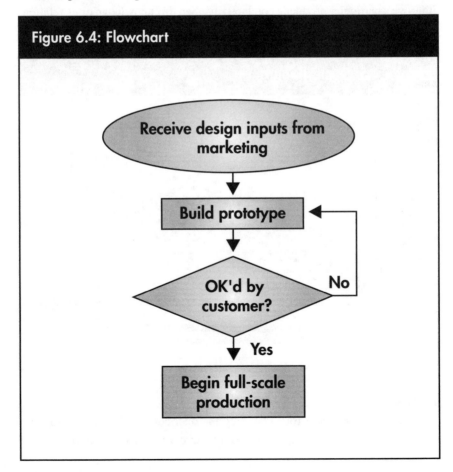

Figure 6.4: Flowchart

Scatter diagram

This is a method for exploring the relationship between two variables within a process. The diagram is constructed of a scaled X and Y axis, both of which represent a variable. The variables could be two qualities assumed to be related in some way: size vs. strength; finish luster vs. durability; speed vs. customer satisfaction; price vs. sales volume. One of the variables is plotted on one axis, and the other on the alternate axis. Unlike a run chart, no attempt is made to illustrate the chronology of data points. The scatter diagram simply provides a snapshot of the two variables over some period of time. The relationship between them becomes clearer as the number of data points are increased. Exploring relationships is an important part of determining or verifying a problem's root cause. In Figure 6.5, a positive relationship exists between the two variables: outer diameter (OD) and conductivity. In other words, as outer diameter increases, so does conductivity. If you're trying to improve a particular product's conductivity, then this knowledge of its relationship to OD will facilitate your efforts.

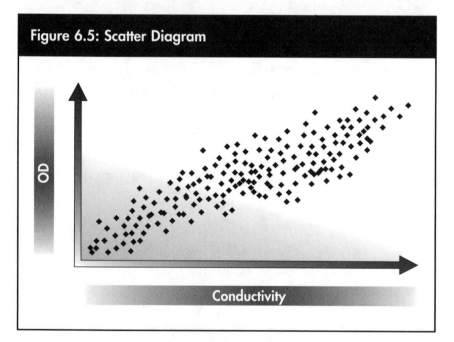

Figure 6.5: Scatter Diagram

Histogram

This is a graphic tool for illustrating the distribution of readings around a target's value. For example, if you manufacture a product with a diameter of exactly two inches, then a histogram will indicate how close you're coming to the target and what the distribution of readings around the target looks like. Histograms begin to indicate something about a process's capability, but they only indicate the shape of the distribution, nothing about the true capability of the process producing the distribution. However, the shape can reveal a great deal about the nature of the process. In Figure 6.6, the process is producing a distribution that resembles a traditional bell-shaped curve—i.e., most readings falling on target, with some gradually tailing off on both sides. This distribution suggests that the process might be in control but additional work would be needed to determine this for sure.

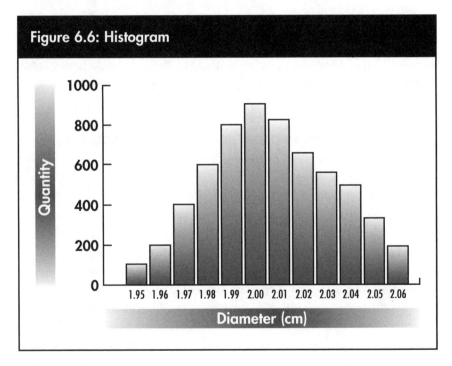

Figure 6.6: Histogram

Selling skills

These comprise another set of the soft tools that most people don't consider part of the problem-solving toolbox. They're absolutely essential to the problem-solving process, particularly when a solution is being presented to decision makers for support. Even the best solution must be sold effectively before it's accepted and implemented. Here are some of the fundamentals of effectively selling an idea or solution:

■ *Sell the benefit to the audience.* Carefully determine ahead of time how the solution will benefit the people you're presenting to. Build the sales pitch around the direct benefits to the audience members.

■ *Provide alternative solutions.* Explain why your solution is superior to the alternatives. Be specific.

■ *Outline a project plan to the decision makers.* Show that the effective path has already been determined; all you need is the go-ahead.

■ *Practice the presentation ahead of time.* A confident, smooth delivery will pave the way to your proposal's acceptance.

■ *Make eye contact with everyone in the room.* Speak as if you're addressing each person individually.

Each of the tools described above are relatively simple to apply. The trick is to use them as widely and as often as possible. Personnel must be reminded of the tools and how they fit into the broader problem-solving method. With constant reinforcement over time, their use will become second nature.

DOS AND DON'TS OF EFFECTIVE PROBLEM SOLVING

Keep these imperatives in mind as you design and implement your system for effective problem solving:

✔ *Do adopt a structured problem-solving method.* Research the many methods in existence and consider customizing one to your organization. Reinforce the problem-solving method through constant reminders and examples of how it works. Provide a lot of practice opportunities.

✔ *Do get people involved.* Include as many people in the problem-solving process as possible. Focus especially on people who have first-hand knowledge of the issues, regardless of their position within the organization.

✔ *Do develop a user-friendly corrective and preventive action system.* If the system is complex and bureaucratic, nobody will use it. Make your system as streamlined as possible. Benchmark systems from other companies and borrow liberally.

✔ *Do put someone in charge of your corrective and preventive action system.* A system as critical as this must have an effective administrator. The person should be organized, respected, and not afraid of ruffling feathers if the need arises.

✔ *Do assign a project manager to every problem.* This person will be responsible for managing the problem-solving process from start to finish. Make sure the person assigned knows that he or she has been assigned.

✔ *Do document your problem-solving process.* Write a procedure or flow diagram to guide the use of your problem-solving method and your corrective and/or preventive action system.

✔ *Do use simple tools to drive problem solving.* Don't try to impress yourself or your employees with complex analytical tools. Simple tools often are the most effective at getting to the root cause of problems.

✘ *Don't assume an understanding of root cause.* A huge mistake is assuming that employees understand what the term root cause means. Explain the concept and give concrete examples of what is and isn't a root cause.

✘ *Don't accept weak or invalid root causes.* When faced with inaccurate root causes, diplomatically return the corrective or preventive action back to the project manager and explain why the response is inadequate. You might have to use the root cause worksheet to drill down to the underlying issues.

✘ *Don't rush the process.* Don't assign arbitrary time limits for how quickly problems must be solved (e.g., "Corrective and preventive actions must be closed within thirty days of initiation"). Some problems take longer than others. Rushing the process will only hamstring its effectiveness.

✘ *Don't include negativity.* Avoid making the problem-solving process a channel for assigning blame and disciplining employees. Nothing will thwart continual improvement more than this.

✘ *Don't neglect vigorous communication.* The organization must communicate about problem solving—its successes, failures, champions, and the contributions of team members—at every possible opportunity. Few communication topics are as important as problem solving within the organization. The more people hear about it, the more they'll feel comfortable with problem solving and their roles within the process.

Chapter Six Appendix

CORRECTIVE AND PREVENTIVE ACTION PROCEDURE

1. Purpose/scope

The procedure's objective is to provide for:

- Initiation
- Root cause investigation
- Action
- Follow-up and closure
- Record keeping and tracking of nonconformities, potential nonconformities, and improvement opportunities that relate to the organization's success.

Correct implementation of this procedure is expected to lead to fewer problems and/or defects, lower costs, and higher profits. The guidelines set forth in this document cover all company locations. Any questions should be directed to the quality manager.

2. Definitions

2.1. *Corrective action:* An action initiated to remove the root cause of an individual nonconformity.

2.2. *Preventive action:* An action initiated to remove the root cause of a potential nonconformity. Improvement opportunities are considered preventive actions because improvements inevitably prevent the erosion of competitive advantage and loss of customers.

2.3. *Corrective/preventive action request form:* Used to record and track corrective actions, preventive actions, and improvement opportunities.

2.4. *Corrective/preventive action administrator:* The individual responsible for ensuring the overall functioning of the corrective and preventive action system. The assistant general manager serves as the corrective/preventive action administrator.

2.5. *Project manager:* The individual responsible for managing the investigation of, and action on, a particular opportunity.

2.6. *Root cause:* The core reason (actionable by the organization) that a nonconformity or potential nonconformity exists.

3. Initiating actions

3.1. Any employee can initiate a corrective or preventive action.

3.2. Corrective actions are triggered by existing nonconformities. Preventive actions are triggered by potential nonconformities or improvement opportunities.

3.3. A corrective or preventive action is initiated by completing the top portion of a corrective/preventive action request form, providing as much detail as possible about the nonconformity, potential nonconformity, or improvement opportunity. Improvement opportunities are noted as preventive actions.

3.4. The corrective/preventive action request form is forwarded to the quality manager, who will evaluate the issue and authorize the form. In the event that an action isn't authorized, the initiator is contacted and a reason is provided.

3.5. Upon authorization, the corrective or preventive action is submitted to the corrective/preventive action administrator for inputting into the tracking database. A project manager and response date are also assigned at this time and recorded on the corrective/preventive action request form. (Project manager is indicated in the space labeled "assigned to.") The project manager is contacted via phone, e-mail, or in person to discuss the assignment.

4. Investigation and action

4.1. The project manager will assemble the necessary personnel and resources to investigate the corrective or preventive action.

4.2. Team-based problem solving will be employed whenever possible, using the prescribed problem-solving method.

4.3. The root cause will be identified and recorded on the corrective/preventive action request form. Corrective or preventive actions proposed to address the issue will also be recorded.

4.4. The project manager is responsible for reporting the status of the corrective or preventive action to the corrective/preventive action administrator by the response date shown on the form.

4.5. Investigation and action will continue until the project is deemed completed by the project manager. The form is then returned to the corrective/preventive action administrator.

4.6. The corrective/preventive action administrator or his or her designee will update the database for all actions taken on the nonconformity, potential nonconformity, or improvement opportunity.

5. Verifying effectiveness

5.1. The corrective/preventive action administrator or his or her designee will follow up to verify effectiveness and determine the results of actions.

5.2. The results of follow-up will be recorded on the corrective/preventive action request form. The tracking database will also be updated to reflect effectiveness and results of actions.

6. Closure

6.1. Upon satisfactory evaluation of the action on the nonconformity, potential nonconformity, or improvement opportunity, the corrective/preventive action administrator will close the issue. The tracking database will be edited to indicate closure.

6.2. Copies of the closed corrective/preventive action request form must be forwarded to the appropriate process manager, business group manager, and the company president.

7. Analysis

7.1. The tracking database maintained by the corrective/preventive action administrator can be used to identify trends, compile summaries, and provide inputs into business review and other meetings, as appropriate.

CA/PA Request Form

Tracking No. ___

Type (check one):

❏ Corrective action ❏ Preventive action

Source (check one):

❏ Customer complaint ❏ Continual improvement idea ❏ Supplier problem

❏ Business review ❏ Audit nonconformity ❏ Info & data analysis

❏ Production problem ❏ Other: _____

Problem or Opportunity Info (attach additional information if necessary):

Location: _____ Date: ___/___/___ Authorized by: _____

Problem/opportunity: _____

_____

_____

_____

_____

Issued to: _____ Response due date: ___/___/___

Investigation & Action (attach additional sheets if necessary):

Root cause: _____

_____

_____

_____

_____

Action taken: _____

_____

_____

_____

_____

Completed by: _____ Date: ___/___/___ Estimated date of completion: ___/___/___

Follow-Up & Closure:

Reviewed by: _____ Date: ___/___/___

Results of action taken: _____

_____

_____

_____

_____ Date closed: ___/___/___

Root Cause Worksheet

Definition of problem:

Superficial cause (i.e., the cause most closely identifiable to the symptom):

1. Why did this happen?

2. Why did this happen?

3. Why did this happen?

4. Why did this happen?

5. Why did this happen?

Root cause:

Date: ___/___/___ CA/PA reference No.: _____

Participants:

Chapter Seven

High-Impact Auditing

In This Chapter
- Requirements vs. Opinions
- Objective Evidence
- Auditing Strategic Processes
- Verification and Closure

nternal auditing can be one of the most effective tools for triggering the continual improvement process. But it can also be an expensive waste of time and a cause of frustration and conflict. The results depend on how an organization plans and manages its audit system. Before we examine the success factors of an audit system, let's define exactly what we mean by internal auditing.

Internal auditing is the process by which an organization examines its ability to meet requirements of a standard such as ISO 9001, conform with internal procedures and commitments, and produce effective results. Auditing is a balanced process, identifying positive and negative aspects of the organization's performance. It's also a planned activity where the auditors and auditees agree on the time, place, and scope of audits. Surprise audits aren't necessary or desired. Internal audits generally use the organization's own personnel as auditors, though occasionally outsiders are called in.

Internal audits offer huge benefits, both to the organization's top management and to auditors themselves:

■ Top managers find out what's really going on within the organization, which gives them a more objective basis for decision making.

■ Top management learns of potential problems before they explode into significant risks.

■ Top management learns where failures are taking place and can initiate containment and corrective action.

■ Top management identifies where resources should be directed.

■ Top management learns how effective training efforts are.

■ Top management learns which processes and personnel are particularly effective.

■ Internal auditors are exposed to other parts of the organization, which broadens their experience and makes them better employees.

■ Internal auditors are exposed to best practices that they can take back to their own areas and implement.

■ Internal auditors learn that they have an effect on the organization and its success, which increases motivation and employee retention.

■ As more employees get experience as internal auditors, the entire organization expands its competency and knowledge base.

For the internal audit system to be effective, it must work in concert with other systems, especially the corrective and preventive action systems. An internal audit takes a snapshot of the organization, identifying nonconformities, opportunities for improvement, and positive practices. It's then up to the corrective and preventive action systems, led by the auditees, to ensure that issues are investigated, causes are identified, actions taken, and results verified. In the case of positive findings, the preventive action system ensures that the positive practices are adopted throughout the organization. The internal audit system doesn't propose specific actions, fixes, solutions, or recommendations. These are the responsibility of the auditees, not the auditors. The auditors simply identify where failures and successes are taking place. By their very nature, audits typically identify more failures than successes, and these failures are what we'll call audit nonconformities.

REQUIREMENTS VS. OPINIONS

Audit nonconformities serve as important raw material for the continual improvement process. To initiate a nonconformity, you must have a requirement; a nonconformity doesn't exist without one. You might have a concern, a remark, an opportunity, or something else, but it won't be a nonconformity without a clear requirement. This fact is lost on many auditors, beginners and experienced alike.

What constitutes an auditable requirement? There are many sources:

- Quality policy, mission statement, or vision
- Quality manual
- Key measures or other measurable objectives
- Job procedures and work instructions
- Lab procedures and test methods
- Product specifications
- Engineering drawings and blueprints
- Process standards, setups, and run sheets
- Inspection checklists
- Maintenance checklists
- Sales orders and contracts
- Job travelers, work orders, and job orders
- Purchase orders
- Records of corrective and preventive actions
- Records of management or business review
- Statutory and regulatory requirements related to the product
- Blank forms, particularly when they include instructions for recording data or carrying out tasks
- Competency and training requirements—often defined within job descriptions and similar documents
- Verbal statements from persons of authority and responsibility speaking about areas under their control

All of these might introduce specific requirements that the organization must implement. Any activity, process, or outcome that doesn't meet such requirements is a nonconformity. The auditor's opinions, notions, philosophies, and personal experiences don't constitute requirements. When people audit with an eye toward driving continual improvement, there's sometimes a tendency for requirements to be invented, usually with very good intentions. Well intended or not, requirements can never be invented. One of the best techniques to ensure that audit nonconformities are written correctly is to insist that they're written in two parts:

- *Requirement.* Exactly what the organization has committed itself to doing
- *Finding.* Exactly what the organization has done that contradicts the commitment stated in the requirement

When nonconformities are written clearly and correctly, they form one of the best inputs to the continual improvement process. When they're not written correctly, confusion and dissension typically result. Veteran auditors are frequently guilty of writing unclear and incorrect nonconformities. They allow their experience to cloud their judgment of what's a requirement and what's an opinion. When faced with an issue that appears to be a problem, all auditors must ask themselves, "What's the requirement that makes this a problem?" This question will ensure that irrelevant or erroneous issues don't get raised.

OBJECTIVE EVIDENCE

Objective evidence consists of a factual recounting of what was seen, heard, or experienced during the audit. Gathering objective evidence comprises the largest dedication of time and effort during an audit. Ideally, the evidence should show that the organization conformed with relevant standards, followed its procedure, and achieved effective outcomes (e.g., customer satisfaction, progress against key measures, or continual improvement). More often, audits identify where the organization failed to meet requirements, and these failures become nonconformities. The organization shouldn't fear or discourage non-conformity reports; they trigger the continual improvement process and facilitate long-term success.

Objective evidence is recorded in the finding portion of the requirement/finding nonconformity format and describes exactly how the organization failed to fulfill the requirement.

Objective evidence meets three criteria:

■ *It's not subject to bias or prejudice.* Auditors can't allow their personal feelings to influence how they interpret evidence or evaluate conformance.

■ *It's traceable.* This means that the issue can be traced to its source. Traceability requires recording as many identifiers as possible, including date, time, function, process, machine, customer, order number, and product code.

■ *It's expressed in the most streamlined and simple manner possible.* Sometimes, auditors will provide a paragraph or more of detail, thinking that the more they write, the more convincing the evidence will be. In reality, the best objective evidence is stated in prose that is simple, streamlined, and to the point.

Objective evidence is stated in such a way that it directly contradicts the requirement stated in the first half of the nonconformity. Enough detail is provided to facilitate traceability, but not so much that it overwhelms. Auditors should remember that auditees are their customers. One of the first products these customers will receive is concise and clearly written findings.

It's useful to examine some examples of correct and incorrect audit write-ups.

Correct

Requirement: The general manager stated that all employees are expected to understand the facility's key measures and how they as employees should contribute to them. (The requirement comes from the general manager's statements, which have the weight of a requirement when he's talking about something under his control.)

Finding: Three out of five employees sampled at random in the shipping department didn't have an understanding of the facility's key measures or how they as employees should contribute to them. (The language of the finding mirrors that of the requirement, stating exactly how the organization failed to meet its commitment. The sample size is defined, as is the location. The employees' names are appropriately omitted to depersonalize the issue as much as possible.)

Incorrect

Requirement: All employees should understand key measures. (It isn't clear whether this is an opinion or a requirement. Where did this "should" come from?)

Finding: Employees were ignorant of the organization's objectives and strategic direction, and they were obviously unprepared to assist in continual improvement. (The overall tone of finding is subjective and accusatorial. It focuses on people, not the system. Also, the finding's wording doesn't mirror the requirement. The sample size and other identifiers are left out, which provides insufficient traceability.)

Correct

Requirement: The business review procedure (Document No. M-05-01, rev. two) states in section 3.2 that, "Inputs to the business review meeting must include the following... (b) customer feedback." (The exact source of the requirement is stated clearly, even down to the document number, revision, and section. Irrelevant information is appropriately omitted and replaced with ellipses.)

Finding: Records of the business review meeting of February 12, 2003, didn't list customer feedback as an input to the meeting. (The finding defines which meeting we're talking about. It will be easy for the organization to locate and investigate the issue, based on the information provided. Again, the wording directly contradicts the commitment in the requirement.)

Incorrect

Requirement: Business reviews must provide leadership in the improvement of customer satisfaction by reviewing customer feedback. (No attribution is given for this requirement. Where did it come from? The statement has the tone of an invented requirement, despite the fact that it could have been extracted from a real requirement.)

Finding: Business reviews are ineffective for the purpose of improving customer satisfaction. (A very subjective statement, one that's bound to create controversy. How did the auditors arrive at this conclusion? What specific evidence was uncovered during the audit? What are the facts? This finding sounds like an opinion, and a potentially controversial one at that.)

Correct

Requirement: The quality policy (rev. of March 30, 2002) states in the second bullet, "Recognizing the strategic importance of our customers' time, we will continually improve our delivery performance." (The requirement is pulled verbatim from its source. Identifiers of policy revision and location within the policy is provided.)

Finding: The logistics manager produced a report titled "Shipping Performance, Year to Date, June 2003," showing that delivery performance had gotten progressively worse during the past six months. (The evidence and source are stated in clear, unambiguous terms.)

Incorrect

Requirement: The quality policy commits to improving delivery performance. (This is a factual statement, but insufficient traceability is provided.)

Finding: The auditors spoke to the logistics manager, who indicated he strongly supported the issues detailed in the quality policy. He stated that all employees were instructed to support the policy through behaviors that lead to its achievement. When asked if his department could provide proof of achieving the quality policy, the logistics manager produced a report showing that instead of getting better, delivery performance had actually gotten worse during the past six months. The logistics manager tried to blame this condition on other functions of the company, stating, "We're doing the best we can do with the resources we're given." He refused to provide details of what resources hadn't been provided. The logistics manager then took an urgent phone call from customer service about a late order, which only reinforced the impression of deteriorating delivery performance and an inability to deploy the quality policy fully. (The auditor decided to write a book about the finding. This doesn't make the evidence stronger. On the contrary, it makes it weaker. The same message could be conveyed in significantly fewer words. Besides being very long and wordy, the finding also has the tone of a personal attack on the logistics manager. The core issue is that the organization has committed to improving delivery performance, and they've failed to do so. Simply tell it like it is.)

The lead auditor or audit manager must continually monitor his or her auditors to ensure that nonconformities are written correctly. It generally takes a number of audits before an inexperienced auditor can confidently draw conclusions from objective evidence and write nonconformities in a clear, concise manner. Auditing practice with experienced auditors is time well spent.

THE SYSTEM, NOT THE PEOPLE

Auditing evaluates the system, not the people. However, one of the best ways to understand the system and its effectiveness is through the people within the organization. After all, people provide a living snapshot of the system in action: the way they receive and interpret information, the manner in which they carry out instructions, the conformity of goods and services they produce, and their effectiveness in satisfying customers. Despite the fact that much objective evidence is obtained from people, the audit's focus remains on the system itself. That's why, when writing nonconformities, employee titles are substituted for employee names.

Some auditees might suspect that the audit process constitutes a personal attack on their jobs or an attempt to get them in trouble. Auditors must be prepared for that reaction. When people act as if they suspect malicious intent, auditors should calmly explain that the audit process is all about the system. Auditors must be able to put the auditees at ease and depersonalize the process as much as possible. If people are uneasy about the audit process, they won't be able to provide objective evidence, and the audit won't trigger the continual improvement process.

Does this mean that people never make mistakes? No, of course not. People make mistakes, all the time. However, when failures are identified during an audit, they're failures of the system. Few audit nonconformities occur because of willful misconduct on an employee's part. If someone makes a mistake or fails to carry out a job step, it's usually because the overall system is flawed and error prone. Fix the system, and people won't have the opportunity to make mistakes.

AUDITING STRATEGIC PROCESSES

Not all organizational processes have the same strategic significance. An internal audit system oriented toward continual improvement of the organization's overall performance will focus on strategic issues. It's worth noting that most management system standards, such as ISO 9001, require audits to be scheduled on the basis of status, importance, and prior audits results. This means, among other things, that business processes with high status and importance (i.e., more strategic importance) will be audited more often.

Specifically, what business processes have high strategic importance? Here are a few that stand out:

Customer satisfaction

How does the organization determine customer requirements and expectations?

How are requirements and expectations communicated throughout the organization?

How are the requirements and expectations converted to products?

What methods are used for capturing customer perceptions about products?

Who is involved in capturing perceptions, and how well do they understand their roles?

How are data on customer perceptions reported and analyzed?

■ Is action taken on what the organization learns from analysis?

Has overall customer satisfaction improved?

Continual improvement

■ Corrective and preventive action
- ❑ Are systems properly and widely used?
- ❑ Is a structured problem-solving method understood and used by personnel?
- ❑ Does proof exist that the root or potential root causes have been identified?
- ❑ Are actions taken to eliminate root or potential root causes?
- ❑ Are actions verified to ensure they were effective?
- ❑ Are data on corrective and preventive actions reported and analyzed?

■ Internal auditing
  ❏ Does audit scheduling clearly reflect the strategic importance of processes and the results of previous audits?
  ❏ Are all the organization's processes and/or functions audited within a reasonable time frame, generally defined as a year?
  ❏ Does top management take corrective action on the nonconformities raised by audits?
  ❏ Do the corrective actions appear to be effective, based on the evidence?

Leadership
■ Has the organizational mission been determined?
■ Has strategy been developed?
■ Have appropriate metrics (i.e., key measures) been selected?
■ Has organizational performance and direction been communicated throughout the organization?
■ Has top management led the review and action on key measures and other important information that indicates organizational success?
■ Has progress been made on improving key measures?

Design and development
■ Is design and development planned in a deliberate and documented manner?
■ Are design inputs and outputs recorded and approved?
■ Is progress against the design plan periodically reviewed?
■ Is the design output verified against input requirements?
■ Is the output of the design process validated under conditions of application or use?

Transformation/production
■ How is work planned and scheduled?
■ What information defines the nature of the products produced?
■ What information guides the performance of work in general?
■ How do personnel understand their job requirements?
■ What sort of verification methods are used?
■ How do personnel receive feedback on their work output?
■ Do personnel understand how their efforts affect key measures?

These audit questions are only examples and might not be applicable to all organizations. Additionally, other processes could have strategic significance, depending on the organization and its competitive environment. Personnel providing audit leadership must examine the various processes within their organization and determine which have the most bearing on the enterprise's long-term success—these processes are the ones that must receive the most scrutiny during audits.

It's worth noting that we've focused on auditing *processes*. Examining processes instead of isolated activities or functions sheds light on the organization's true effectiveness. Many activities appear effective when viewed in isolation but are much less so when examined in the broader context of their processes.

TRAINING AUDITORS

The audit function's success depends on auditor training. Many audits produce poor results because auditors simply don't know what they're doing. It's not their fault. They haven't received proper instruction or been given opportunities to practice what they've learned. An organization must invest time and effort in making its auditors competent and confident before they're ever assigned to an audit.

What are the elements of effective auditor training? Auditors must receive instruction about:

- Practical interpretations of the standard that the organization has adopted (e.g., ISO 9001, ISO 14001, ISO/TS 16949)
- The purpose of auditing and how it drives continual improvement (i.e., by providing a balanced picture of the organization and triggering corrective and/or preventive actions)
- The audit phases and various activities within each phase (e.g., scheduling, planning, on-site auditing, reporting, and follow-up)
- Sources of audit requirements (e.g., the standard, procedures, and other sources)
- Methods of gathering objective evidence and drawing valid conclusions
- Diplomacy skills and effective interpersonal communication
- Audit role-playing under controlled conditions
- Writing nonconformities in the prescribed format
- Actual auditing with an experienced auditor

Auditor training doesn't necessarily need to be formal or even classroom-based. Training style and format will differ significantly from one organization to the next. However, all auditors must have a conceptual understanding of the process and a practical grasp of techniques, both supported by plenty of practice. When auditors understand their roles and responsibilities, the audit process is more likely to contribute to strategic continual improvement.

A successful audit process always includes an individual who takes personal ownership in the process. He or she may be the quality manager, quality assurance supervisor, or lead auditor; the title is unimportant. The person must be able to carry out five complex and linked activities, all of which contribute to the audit process's desired objective. Let's examine each of these activities and explore how they fit together.

AUDIT SCHEDULING

An audit schedule defines the auditing that will take place over an extended period of time, usually six months or a year. The purpose of the schedule is twofold:

■ Communicate to the audit team when its services will be needed and where
■ Communicate to the auditee when an audit will be scheduled and what it will require

As explained earlier, surprise audits aren't necessary or desired, and the audit schedule helps ensure that everyone is on the same page. Audits scheduled far in advance with plenty of preliminary communications always produce better results.

The schedule reflects which processes are considered more strategically important by how frequently they're audited. Processes and functions that have performed poorly in previous audits are also scheduled more often. Because the schedule is based on considerations such as importance and previous audit performance, the schedule itself is revised regularly as circumstances change. Regardless of other considerations, all processes, functions, and departments within the scope of the management system must be audited at least once a year.

The schedule can be keyed to organizational processes, departments, functions, facilities, ISO standard elements, or some other aspect. However, it must communicate clearly to auditors and auditees alike what audits are coming up and when. Audit schedules provide just enough detail to guide the process and facilitate the next logical step: audit planning. A sample audit schedule is shown in this chapter's appendix, on page 112.

AUDIT PLANNING

An audit schedule defines the audit process over an extended time frame, but an audit plan is much more focused, detailing a single audit's scope and objectives. An audit plan provides a chronology of the audit from start to finish: what processes will be audited and when, who will be doing the auditing, what requirements will be audited in each segment of the audit. Even details such as meetings, breaks, and lunches are shown on the audit plan. Everything is laid out in as much detail as possible. The audit plan has two primary purposes:

■ To clear up any timing conflicts between auditees and auditors
■ To keep the audit on track by giving everyone a detailed plan to follow

The audit plan is typically distributed several days before the audit. It's common for auditees to request alterations to the plan based on existing logistics and commitments. By all means, modify it to accommodate auditees. The plan's only fixed attribute is audit scope—except under extreme circumstances, such as acts of God or employee accidents. When possible, the lead auditor should solicit changes prior to the audit's start, but sometimes the auditee will request changes right up to the opening meeting or later.

AUDIT SUPERVISION

The audit's on-site portion consists primarily of gathering evidence. The lead auditor takes part in this, of course, but he or she must also manage the overall process. These duties include:

■ Leading the opening meeting
■ Managing and communicating changes to the audit plan as needed
■ Ensuring that the audit stays on track, covering all required processes and/or functions within the allotted time
■ Ensuring that auditors remain objective and unbiased, evaluating all evidence in a consistent manner
■ Encouraging auditors to write up their positive observations and nonconformities during the course of the audit (during breaks and lunches) so there's no time crunch directly before the closing meeting
■ Reviewing all nonconformities written by audit team members to ensure that they're logical, valid, and clearly written
■ Providing feedback to audit team members on their performance so that individuals can target areas for their own development and improvement
■ Resolving conflicts in a constructive manner, whether they're within the audit team or between auditors and auditees

- Keeping the auditee apprised of the audit's progress on an ongoing basis
- Leading the closing meeting that presents audit results
- Ensuring that the entire process is conducted in a polished, professional manner with a positive overall tone

If these duties sound difficult, it's because they are. Many organizations have ineffective audit processes because their so-called lead auditors don't understand their responsibilities. An accredited, five-day lead auditor course is a good investment for those individuals who hope to function as their organization's lead auditor. The role can't be taken lightly.

AUDIT REPORTING

The first formal reporting that occurs during an audit is the closing meeting. The meeting is lead by the lead auditor and presents a verbal summary of the audit, including positives and negatives. Depending on the audit's size and duration, the closing meeting might last from fifteen minutes to more than an hour. The closing meeting is interactive, allowing dialogue between auditors and auditees. During the closing meeting, the auditee is typically presented with the written audit observations and/or corrective action requests, and these can also form the basis for the discussion of audit results.

Subsequent to the closing meeting, and occasionally during it, an audit report is presented to the auditee. The report summarizes the audit at a high level, describing overall themes and trends revealed by the audit. It's usually written by the lead auditor and draws from evidence gathered by the entire audit team during the audit. The report doesn't rehash every single audit observation, this has already been addressed during the closing meeting. Audit reports must be as concise and streamlined as possible; nobody wants to read a book about the audit. Graphics such as matrices and Pareto diagrams are helpful in facilitating the auditee's understanding of the overall results.

VERIFICATION AND CLOSURE

The auditee is asked to respond to audit nonconformities by an agreed date after the audit. The response will include investigation into root cause, proposals for corrective action, and another date by which the auditee commits to completing these actions. Sometimes, the response also includes corrective action already taken, but more often it's simply proposed. The response date could be within a few days or a number of weeks, but it's agreed upon during the closing meeting.

The lead auditor reviews the auditee's responses to determine whether the investigation and proposed corrective action are adequate. This is the first stage of verification. Specifically, the responses are reviewed for the following attributes:

- An identifiable viable root cause, as opposed to a restatement of the symptoms. (Refer to chapter six for a detailed explanation of root cause analysis.)
- A proposed corrective action that relates logically to the identified root cause.

One of the most important jobs that the lead auditor and his or her team can perform is a careful scrutiny of auditee responses. Accepting weak investigations and/or corrective actions doesn't help anyone and certainly doesn't trigger continual improvement. In the event that a response doesn't identify a plausible root cause or propose a corrective action related to it, the lead auditor must *diplomatically* reject the response and explain to the auditee why it's inadequate. Note the emphasis on the word "diplomatically" because the auditee is always the customer of the audit process. Treat this customer with the same respect that any other customer would receive.

The second stage of verification occurs when the auditee notifies the lead auditor that corrective action has been implemented. At this stage, the lead auditor or audit team member will verify that the following criteria have been met:

- Full implementation of the corrective action proposed by the auditee
- Evidence that the root cause of the original nonconformity has been eliminated

Sometimes verification is performed through a review of records or documents submitted by the auditee. At other times it's performed through an on-site visit to review evidence. The nonconformity's nature and significance generally will determine whether on-site verification is necessary.

Once all audit nonconformities have been addressed with effective corrective action, the audit is considered closed. However, the fact that it's closed doesn't mean it's forgotten. A high-level discussion of audit results is an important input to the business review process, and the trends identified by audits influence the allocation of resources and strategic decision making.

DOS AND DON'TS OF AUDITING FOR CONTINUAL IMPROVEMENT

Internal auditing is one of the best processes an organization can use to drive continual improvement. Keep the following dos and don'ts in mind as your organization implements and improves its system of internal auditing:

✔ *Do insist that auditors use the requirement/finding format.* This format helps ensure that a requirement exists before a nonconformity is raised.

✔ *Do recruit a wide variety of personnel as internal auditors.* The broader the range of auditors, the richer the perspectives and experiences that will be brought to the process.

✔ *Do assign a competent person to lead internal audits.* A responsible individual must be assigned ownership for the audit process and manage all aspects of it in an effective manner.

✔ *Do schedule audits based on strategic importance.* Audit processes scheduled by strategic importance and the results of previous audits will contribute the most to the organization's success.

✔ *Do keep the audit process professional and positive.* Audits must be conducted with professionalism so that personnel understand the process's importance. Audits should also have a positive tone, even if what they reveal is negative.

✘ *Don't allow invented requirements.* With the best intentions, auditors sometimes invent requirements. This corrupts the process and confuses personnel.

✘ *Don't propose actions or fixes to auditees.* Investigating nonconformities and taking corrective action are the auditees' responsibilities. Avoid suggesting or implying any kind of fix related to audit findings.

✘ *Don't neglect auditor training and experience.* The audit process will only be as effective as the weakest auditor. Make sure to provide comprehensive training to all auditors, along with plenty of practice for sharpening skills and judgment.

✘ *Don't allow an audit to assign blame.* Keep the audit focused on the system, not people. Make sure that audit nonconformities are written so that that they don't cast blame.

Chapter Seven Appendix

Yellowjacket Technologies—Internal Audit Schedule

Approved by Craig Cochran
Date: Jan 4, 20XX

LEGEND:
Scheduled = x
Audit conducted = 0
Closed-out = $

Process to be audited	ISO 9001 elements to be addressed	January	February	March	April	May	June	July	August	September	October	November	December
Leadership process*	4.1, 5.1, 5.2, 5.3, 5.4, 5.5, 5.6, 6.1, 7.1, 8.1, 8.4, 8.5			$						x			
Customer satisfaction and order-fulfillment process*	5.4.1, 7.2.1, 7.2.2, 7.2.3, 8.2.1, 8.4			$						x			
Inbound process	4.2.3, 4.2.4, 5.4.1, 7.1, 7.4.1, 7.4.2, 7.4.3, 7.5.1, 7.5.3, 7.5.5										x		
Outbound process	4.2.3, 4.2.4, 5.4.1, 7.5.1, 7.5.3, 7.5.5					$							
Plant No. 1 transformation process*	4.2.3, 4.2.4, 5.4.1, 6.3, 6.4, 7.1, 7.5.1, 7.5.2, 7.5.3, 7.5.4, 7.5.5, 7.6, 8.2.3, 8.2.4, 8.3, 8.5		$							x			
Plant No. 2 transformation process*	4.2.3, 4.2.4, 5.4.1, 6.3, 6.4, 7.1, 7.5.1, 7.5.2, 7.5.3, 7.5.4, 7.5.5, 7.6, 8.2.3, 8.2.4, 8.3, 8.5	$					$						
Maintenance process	4.2.3, 4.2.4, 5.4.1, 6.3, 6.4, 7.5.1, 7.6, 8.2.3									x			
Corrective and preventive action process*	4.2.3, 4.2.4, 8.5					$		0					
Internal audit process*	4.2.3, 4.2.4, 6.2, 8.2.2, 8.5		$				$						
Competency and training	4.2.3, 4.2.4, 6.2											x	
Calibration	4.2.3, 4.2.4, 6.3, 6.4, 7.6								0				

* = Processes determined to have higher strategic importance

Internal Audit Plan

Yellowjacket Technologies—September 15, 20XX

Scope: Leadership process, customer satisfaction and order-fulfillment processes, maintenance process, and plant No. 1 transformation processes

Objective: To drive continual improvement and prepare for the upcoming external audit by our third-party registrar

Wednesday, Sept. 15, 20XX

7:00–7:30 AM
Audit Team Meeting
7:30–7:45 AM
Opening Meeting
7:45—8:30 AM

Team 1 (CC, SC)	Team 2 (PC, EH)
Leadership process including ISO 9001 elements 4.1, 5.1, 5.2, 5.3, 5.4, 5.5, 5.6, 6.1, 7.1, 8.1, 8.4, and 8.5	Customer satisfaction and order-fulfillment processes including ISO 9001 elements 7.2.1, 7.2.2, 7.2.3, 8.2.1, and 8.4

8:30—10:00 AM	
Plant No. 1 transformation process with warehousing, shipping, and receiving including ISO 9001 elements 6.3, 6.4, 7.1, 7.5.1, 7.5.2, 7.5.3, 7.5.4, 7.5.5, 7.6, 8.2.3, 8.2.4, 8.3, and 8.5	Maintenance process including ISO 9001 elements 6.3, 6.4, 7.5.1, 7.6, and 8.2.3

10:00—11:00
Auditor Review Meeting
11:00—11:30
Closing Meeting and Q&A
11:30+
Adjourn

Auditors

Paolo Chiappina (PC), Auditor • Steve Cowart (SC), Auditor • Ed Hardison (EH), Auditor • Craig Cochran (CC), Lead Auditor

Auditor notes

1. Please write-up your audit observations as you go! There's not a whole lot of time for closing meeting prep so we'll need to keep up with things as we go along.

2. Be on the lookout for any positive practices that can be highlighted.

3. Make sure to audit key measures in every process that you enter.

Chapter Eight

Building a Culture of Continual Improvement

In This Chapter
- Respect
- Involvement
- Communication
- Orderliness
- Recognition

Organizational culture is a difficult concept to grasp. Part of the problem lies with culture's intangibility. Every organization has a culture, but it's hard for most people to see, touch, hear, or smell. Culture is transparent to all but the most astute observer. It exists as if in gaseous form, reaching to every corner of the organization but remaining largely invisible.

The other difficulty with organizational culture is that it's the result of many different things. It's an outcome that's nearly impossible to affect directly. You could never implement a culture the way you would implement a new system or procedure. A specific culture could be cultivated over time, however, by implementing such thing as systems and procedures. Thus, culture is a product of nearly every action and decision that occurs within an organization over many months and years.

How can culture be identified? Despite its complexity, it leaves markers that can be found throughout an organization if you know what to look for. These include, among other issues:

■ The way people treat one another

■ Degree of trust between organizational members

■ Magnitude, breadth, and type of communication

- Values and ethics held by organizational members
- People's general appearance, dress, and demeanor
- Personnel's motivation
- Management's and staff's interest in making improvements and changes
- The amount and type of employee development and training
- Job security
- Dangers or risks in carrying out organization's mission

Organizational culture has an enormous effect on continual improvement efforts. Positive cultures facilitate continual improvement and long-term success. Negative ones facilitate fear, insecurity, suspicion, and sabotage. Somewhere in the middle are cultures that don't inspire much of anything except indifference.

Top management must always be mindful of the culture it's cultivating through day-to-day actions. For better or worse, an organization's leaders are under constant surveillance. Their actions shape the organization's culture, either positively or negatively. Top management can embrace a few simple behaviors that will lead to a strong and positive culture, one that helps drive continual improvement. These are:

- Respect
- Involvement
- Communication
- Orderliness
- Recognition

Simple actions? Yes, simple and profound. These are soft behaviors—the ones that often are perceived as a waste of time by some managers. Actually, they're among the most important issues that management can address.

Let's examine each of these concepts individually and see how they can be applied practically.

RESPECT

Respect is one of the most fundamental interpersonal qualities. It's remarkably simple in practice: Communicate through words and deeds that other people have value, their jobs are important, their ideas have merit, and their personal lives have significance. Simply put, treat people the same way you want to be treated. Respect is the basis for all successful, enduring relationships. You could argue that even love takes a back seat to respect in terms of importance.

All managers agree that respect is important, but putting that agreement into practice is another matter. Managers often do things, usually unconsciously, that indicate a lack of respect for their personnel. Sometimes their actions are intentional. Regardless, the result is the same: unmotivated personnel who couldn't care less about improvement.

Safety

The most profound manifestation of respect is a safe workplace. Unsafe conditions communicate one message loudly and clearly: We don't care about the people here. Unsafe conditions are also very expensive. They threaten the organization's very existence. One of management's most important jobs is to identify ways that people can get hurt and to eliminate the causes of these hazards.

Safety is a huge topic with its own body of knowledge. However, there are some fairly universal safety items that management can investigate and take action on. Here are issues that would appear on nearly any safety checklist:

- Emergency preparedness and response plans written and communicated?
- Evacuation maps posted?
- Emergency phone numbers posted?
- Appropriate lighting in work areas?
- Spills and debris cleaned up promptly?
- Exits marked and unobstructed?
- Accidents and near misses formally investigated?
- Guards on all machines and equipment?
- Chemicals stored and labeled correctly?
- Material safety data sheets available to personnel?
- Personal protective equipment maintained in good repair and used correctly?
- All employees and contractors trained in safety?
- Fire extinguishers available, accessible, and inspected periodically?

Obviously, each organization must tailor its safety inspection checklist to the specific issues it faces. A generic safety checklist is provided in this chapter's appendix, on page 141.

Status differentiators

Another way to make respect part of the organization's culture is to remove status differentiators. These are the trappings of the workplace that let everyone know that some people are better or more important than others. Status differentiators are easy to spot because they have no functional purpose. Here are some examples:

■ *Reserved parking spaces for managers.* The only legitimate reason to reserve parking spaces is to accommodate handicapped persons and to reward people for outstanding performances. A similar differentiator is allowing managers park in front of the facility, and requiring staff to park behind it. The fairest and most respectful parking policy is first-come, first-served.

■ *General office areas that are off-limits to production or hourly employees during business hours.* Locking doors leading into office areas or posting signs prohibiting entrance communicates to employees that they're unsuitable for such a refined environment. It also limits communication, which is contrary to a culture of continual improvement. Please note that I'm not suggesting that all doors be unlocked and access available to all areas; storerooms and hazard areas must, of course, be secured. However, general office areas should be accessible to all during normal business hours.

■ *Uniforms for some employees but not others.* If a uniform is believed to have a positive effect on some employees, why wouldn't it be desirable for all employees? Either make uniforms universal or eliminate them. The only exception would be when uniforms have a special functional purpose unique to certain jobs.

■ *Rewards and compensation that are distributed irrationally and are irrelevant to the organization's success.* The classic example of this is the organization that is performing poorly and losing money but which sees fit to provide bonuses to its executives. At the same time executives are receiving their bonuses, rank-and-file employees are being laid off or facing reduced compensation. If the organization is doing well, everyone should benefit because everyone contributed. If the organization is doing poorly, then everyone should suffer equally.

■ *Taking a personal interest in some employees but not others.* It's very important to take an honest interest in other people's lives. This reinforces the notion that the organization cares about its people. Taking an interest must be done equally, however. It's human nature to like some people more than other people, but this tendency must be overcome if the organization wants build a broad culture of continual improvement. When most employees perceive that management is genuinely interested in their lives (e.g., financial well-being, families, hobbies, or problems), then they are more motivated to contribute to continual improvement. Smart managers cultivate an honest interest in all their personnel, then take the time to demonstrate that interest.

■ *Rigid work rules for some employees but not others.* Many years ago, I worked at a firm that had published a handbook of work rules for its production employees. The rules sounded like they'd been developed in the nineteenth century to manage indentured servants. One of my favorite rules was that you could be fired if you were caught leaving your department and going to another. Never mind that it was often necessary to do so to verify product requirements or receive feedback on quality; you could still be fired. All the production employees lusted over the chance to "cross over the wall" and become an office employee. As you might guess, office employees weren't bound by any work rules. The resentment and frustration expressed by production employees were amazing. Were production employees interested in improving their processes? Of course not. They simply wanted to clock in, do as little as possible during their shifts, and clock out. It was hard for me to blame them.

Keep in mind that some practices may seem like status differentiators but are actually functional imperatives, such as offices that are provided for managers but not for other personnel. In most organizations, managers require offices because the tasks they carry out require privacy and quiet. This makes sense. The organization must evaluate each status issue individually and ask if there's a functional reason for its existence. If not, consider removing it or extending its benefits to everyone. Anything less runs counter to the culture of continual improvement.

INVOLVEMENT

Involvement is the practice of using employees to their fullest. This doesn't mean working them till they drop but rather making full use of everyone's creativity, intellect, resourcefulness, and special skills. Involvement takes planning. Most organizations are very good at assigning specific tasks to their personnel, but they often fall short on using all aspects of their employees.

The more employees are involved in the organization's affairs, the better prepared they are to make meaningful contributions. Adopting a philosophy of involvement doesn't mean embracing communist principles. It simply means committing to managing resources in the most efficient and effective manner possible. When planned correctly, personnel involvement will drive the entire organization's efficiency and effectiveness.

Suggestion systems

One of the most significant ways of involving personnel is by soliciting their suggestions and ideas through suggestion systems. These systems have come and gone (and come again) in most organizations, and they're known by an array of names and acronyms. Their basic structure is simple:

■ Provide a means by which personnel can propose improvements
■ Evaluate the inputs
■ Implement the practical ideas

Suggestion systems are straightforward, so there's no reason they shouldn't succeed everywhere they're implemented. Unfortunately, they're often failures, abandoned after only a few months of use. The reason? The systems aren't properly designed and managed. Let's examine some of the success factors of suggestion systems, starting with the medium used to capture suggestions and input.

Personnel must be provided with a convenient way to record their suggestions and ideas. Usually this is a form of some sort, either hard copy or electronic. It should be as short and simple as possible. Ask only for as much information as is absolutely needed. You don't want to discourage people from providing their ideas and suggestions, and a long, complicated form will certainly do so. Generally, the information needed is:

■ Employee's name
■ Date submitted
■ Location/department/process
■ Idea or suggestion in as much detail as possible

Some people quibble with the idea of asking for the submitter's name, believing this might discourage some people. Possibly, but in all the years I managed a system of this sort, I never heard of it keeping anyone from submitting ideas. On the contrary, having the submitter's name has a number of distinct benefits:

■ Occasionally, it's not completely clear what someone is proposing. Knowing who made the suggestion allows follow-up to clarify the idea or, in some cases, probe the issue further.
■ A name prevents people from using the system incorrectly by submitting gripes, accusations, and the like.
■ A name allows management to recruit the person in implementing the idea or suggestion, when practical. This generates an enormous amount of ownership for the idea's success.

■ The name allows management to inform the person of the results of the suggestion's evaluation. This is the hallmark of a successful system.
■ The name allows management to recognize those who contributed the idea once implementation is complete.

Some suggestion systems ask submitters to estimate the benefit or payoff of their ideas. This is one of the worst things you can ask because it often discourages employees from making suggestions. An organization shouldn't worry about the payoff or benefit. The primary benefit is building a culture of continual improvement. Sure, there will be other quantitative benefits, but there's no reason to estimate them at the onset. The immediate payoff is fostering involvement among all employees.

Hard-copy suggestion cards are probably the most common means for employees to record their suggestions. Another way is to establish a large, erasable-marker board in a central location or within each department or process. When personnel have suggestions or ideas, they can simply walk up to the board and record them for everyone to see. This method certainly has some advantages:

■ Ideas won't get lost in the shuffle, as sometimes happens with cards or forms
■ Ideas receive scrutiny from department peers, which can inspire other ideas and suggestions

After you establish the manner in which suggestions will be recorded, the next step is to define the system's scope. This must be clear to everyone. The more specific you can be, the fewer problems you'll have later on. The most successful suggestion systems focus on what employees know best: their own work processes. The following topics should be considered fair game for ideas and suggestions:

■ Job procedures and methods
■ Sequence of operations
■ Tools and equipment
■ Materials and supplies
■ Supplier and subcontractor performance
■ Production scheduling
■ Product design and/or performance
■ Labeling and packaging
■ Safety

- Housekeeping
- Ergonomics
- Environmental conditions (e.g., lighting, temperature, or humidity)
- Other variables that affect employees' work

Anything that can make employees' jobs easier, smarter, safer, more effective, or more efficient should be within the scope of the suggestion system. The whole point is to get employees involved in improving their processes and anything that affects them. Certain issues, however, aren't appropriate for addressing within the suggestion system. The issues listed below should be brought to a supervisor's attention and addressed individually:

- Gripes
- Accusations
- Rumors
- Grievances
- Personnel issues (e.g., harassment, discrimination, substance abuse, or violence)
- Compensation issues
- Disputes with organizational policy
- Management philosophy

One of the best tactics for educating personnel about the system's scope is to ask everyone to focus on issues of concern to customers, whether internal or external. This will keep inputs from straying too far into the realm of the absurd.

The collection point for ideas and suggestions must be located conveniently for employees. If personnel have computer access, then the collection point might be completely electronic. Hard-copy suggestions can be submitted into some sort of collection box or given directly to supervisors. My personal preference is requiring personnel to give the suggestion forms directly to a supervisor. This allows for prescreening of the suggestions for inappropriate issues and keeps supervisors in the loop. Supervisors will subconsciously—or consciously—kill the suggestion system if they feel it compromises their ability to supervise. They must feel that they're part of the system and not being circumvented by it. After all, its purpose is to improve processes in which supervisors and managers are directly involved.

Suggestions are forwarded directly to a suggestion administrator, who inputs them into a database for tracking purposes, much like corrective and preventive actions. Logging each suggestion into a database prevents any of them from going astray. The administrator also assigns an owner to each suggestion, who is responsible for investigating it further and taking action if appropriate. Occasionally, the assigned owner is actually not the correct person to receive the suggestion. In these cases, the administrator is simply notified, and someone else is assigned. A suggestion's owner has three responsibilities:

■ Investigate the suggestion or idea and assemble appropriate resources to implement it.

■ Brief the administrator about the investigation and action, including the final results.

■ If the person who offered the suggestion isn't involved with implementing it, keep him or her informed about the investigation and action, including the final results.

When the suggestion requires problem solving, it's important to involve the person who offered the suggestion. Typically, he or she will know the most about the problem and its variables. Employees are also the most affected by the issue, so they're motivated to get results. Be careful, though, about involving employees who are reluctant or not trained in the required methods and tools. They should understand what problem solving is before they're asked to participate in a session.

Suggestions are acknowledged in all cases, including the crazy ideas. Acknowledgement doesn't have to be anything more elaborate than telling someone, "Hey, we got your suggestion. Thanks a lot. Unfortunately, cost and practicality won't allow us to put shag carpeting in the production area as you've suggested, but we appreciate the idea. Keep the ideas flowing." People usually don't mind having their ideas turned down if there's a reason for it. However, nobody likes their ideas to disappear into a black hole. The person responsible for acknowledging the suggestion is typically the owner. Besides basic acknowledgment, it's also important to keep people informed of their ideas' progress. Many are long-term in nature; some might even require capital expenditures. In most cases people don't mind waiting for results as long as they know that progress is being made and the issue hasn't been dropped.

Committees shouldn't review suggestions. This only slows the system down and adds unnecessary bureaucracy. Individuals perform quite effectively as suggestion owners. Teams or committees can be assembled at the owner's discretion, of course, but ultimate ownership resides with the individual who's been assigned by the suggestion administrator.

The suggestion administrator has four important roles in managing the system:

■ Faithfully inputting the details of all suggestions and ideas into a database. Generally, this involves assigning a tracking number and owner for each suggestion.

■ Updating the database as progress is made on the suggestion.

■ Motivating action when the investigation is taking too long or when the owner appears to have forgotten about the issue.

■ Preparing statistics on the number of suggestions and their success in implementation. Top management will be curious about the results of the system, and the suggestion administrator is the best person to provide this information.

Your suggestion system is like any other program in the organization: It must be relatively simple and understood by all. It needs daily management, oversight, and visibility. Also, top management must believe in the system. If these conditions are met, then it stands a strong chance of producing impressive results.

One caveat related to suggestion systems: They require time and energy to administer. The investment is repaid many times over, but sometimes the payback is difficult to quantify. Don't embark halfheartedly on implementing a suggestion system. Either be willing to apply the necessary resources over the long term, or forget about the idea altogether. Why? Because beginning a system of this sort, only to abandon it a few months later, lets everybody know that management really doesn't understand or care about continual improvement.

See the sample suggestion form on the following page and the procedure on page 149 in the appendix to this chapter.

Figure 8.1: Sample Suggestion System Card

(Front of Card)

Yellowjacket Technologies

Process Improvement Recommendation

Location: _____ Tracking No.: _____

Name: _____ Date submitted: ___/___/___

Idea, improvement, or problem: _____

_____

_____

_____

_____

_____

Supervisor approval: _____

(Back of Card)

Process Improvement Recommendation (PIR) Form Instructions

1. Write your name, the date, and your idea, improvement, or problem on the front of the PIR card. Ask yourself the questions, "How can my process be improved?" and "What would make my job easier?" Attach drawings or extra description, if necessary.
2. Give the completed PIR card to your supervisor.
3. You'll be notified by your supervisor or department manager about what will be done.

PIR assigned to: _____

Action taken: _____

_____

Completion date: ___/___/___ Completed by: _____

Date response given to employee:___/___/___ Employee signature: _____

Problem-solving teams

Another way to involve personnel is to include them on problem-solving teams. One of the fundamentals of effective problem solving is involving a wide range of personnel. Few activities build a culture of continual improvement faster than allowing personnel to help solve problems that affect them.

The biggest obstacle to involving people in problem-solving teams is that they already have responsibilities that must be carried out, and participating in teams pulls them away from their daily work. But that is a rather narrow view of involvement. To build a true culture of continual improvement, you must broaden your organization's understanding of what constitutes someone's job. Participating in problem-solving teams isn't an extracurricular activity—it's a core responsibility. In organizations that really embrace continual improvement, everyone is expected to assist in problem solving. If management is smart about how individuals are used for this critical function, then the entire organization will become stronger, wiser, and more adaptable.

Employee involvement of this sort is an investment, just like any other investment the organization must make to survive. Keep the following in mind as you begin to use employees in problem-solving teams:

■ *Make sure that everyone has been trained on the problem-solving method and applicable tools prior to joining a team.* There's nothing more frustrating than being asked to participate in something you know nothing about.

■ *Use meeting facilitators, especially at first.* These individuals ensure that the group stays focused, everyone participates, and conflicts are resolved constructively. Facilitators become less necessary as personnel gain experience in the mechanics of team dynamics.

■ *Make sure that everyone understands that participation is required.* Personnel are not allowed to opt out.

■ *Once a team has solved a problem, recognize the participants and disband the team.* Don't allow teams to become social clubs.

■ *Over time, ensure that everyone gets an opportunity to participate.* It's tempting to use the people who are particularly effective problem solvers and to avoid those who are less so. However, if people never have an opportunity to participate, they'll never improve their skills.

Process improvement teams

Very similar to problem-solving teams, improvement teams bring together employees to improve a process. There might not be an existing problem, but the organization wants to anticipate potential trouble and act on it before it becomes an issue.

Improvement teams are excellent ways to involve personnel in the organization's strategic success. However, participants must understand exactly what they're supposed to be improving. Companies are famous for sending their employees to improvement tools training, only to tell them when they return, "OK, now go improve something!" Vague objectives of this sort are nearly impossible to act upon. Teams need specific, focused objectives. The improvement team's scope and objective should be documented and understood by everyone involved.

Another important consideration is that there's only so much "low-hanging fruit." Yes, it's easy to succeed in the early stages of a continual improvement effort. But it's much harder to identify big savings and huge breakthroughs in an organization that's been using improvement teams for some time. In fact, the big breakthroughs often require the application of capital. In other words, management must be willing to spend some money.

Here are the three keys to success with improvement teams:

■ Give them specific, focused objectives. Don't just mandate the vague goal of "making improvements."

■ Don't expect huge cost savings every time an improvement team is established. Small incremental improvements contribute just as much to a culture of continual improvement.

■ Management must be willing to listen to, and act upon, its improvement teams' advice. They shouldn't be shocked if teams recommend capital investment to drive improvements.

Customer interaction

An excellent way to make full use of employees is customer interaction.

Organizational representatives visit customers routinely, but the people who typically participate are sales, technical, or purchasing personnel. Other employees seldom get the opportunity. Involving a wide range of personnel in customer visits offers a number of important benefits:

■ *Personnel observe firsthand how their products are used by the customer.* They see the good, the bad, and the ugly, all from the perspective of those who actually use the product. Most important, personnel begin to understand how their jobs affect customers. Personnel are better equipped to improve their job performance and enhance their own careers.

■ *The organization benefits from personnel who grasp the implications of their performance and its effect on customers.* When personnel return to their jobs, they're better prepared to deliver products that meet customer requirements and expectations. The entire organization develops an appreciation of the customer and a desire to achieve customer satisfaction.

■ *The customer receives the powerful message that the organization cares about its business.* It cares so much, in fact, that it's willing to send its employees on customer visits to view their products' performance. The relationship between customer and supplier is reinforced and enhanced.

The customer visits mentioned above can be part of a system of field reporting, a powerful customer satisfaction tool. (This system is described in detail in my book, *Customer Satisfaction: Tools, Techniques, and Formulas for Success,* Paton Press, 2003.)

COMMUNICATION

Communication lies at the heart of continual improvement. Every topic in this book addresses communication of some description, but two important communication tools haven't been addressed yet: newsletters and effective meetings.

Newsletters

Many organizations establish newsletters to facilitate communication; monthly, bimonthly, or quarterly newsletters are fairly common. These newsletters' usefulness varies widely. Often, producing the newsletter becomes a self-consuming task, requiring hours or days of preparation time. The process gradually becomes more important than the product. Don't let this happen. A newsletter's purpose is to communicate. Puzzles, riddles, trivia, cartoons, and other diversions may or may not communicate anything of value. The same goes for elaborate graphic layouts.

"Brevity is the soul of wit," Shakespeare wrote, and this certainly applies to newsletters. The best are short and sweet; the very best are comprised of a single page, either hard copy or electronic, written in a conversational manner. These are easy to write and distribute. Their simple production requirements allow them to be more timely, appearing as often as once a week. Because they're short, personnel are likely to read and absorb the information. The end result is that everyone begins to understand what's going on within the organization. The more that happens, the better prepared everyone is to contribute to the organization's success.

What types of information should be addressed within a newsletter? Here are a few possibilities:

- Problem-solving successes
- Customer feedback
- Progress toward objectives
- Future challenges
- Personnel changes
- Individual and team successes
- Process improvements
- New products, processes, equipment, or customers

Some of this information could be considered sensitive, appropriate for internal consumption only. To protect the information from being shared outside the organization, simply ask employees to keep the newsletter to themselves. They should protect the information in the newsletter in the same way they'd protect their own personal information. After all, the organization is entrusting them with high-level communications that affect the organization's success and, by extension, the success of employees and their families. Only the most malicious employee would consider passing information along to competitors or other inappropriate parties. The benefits of having a well-informed workforce outweighs the risks of sensitive information being compromised.

Regardless, use common sense when deciding whether to publish sensitive company information. Some issues are better left unpublished.

A sample newsletter is provided in this chapter's appendix, on page 145.

Effective meetings

A culture of continual improvement is founded on getting things done. Unfortunately, when people think of getting things done, the last tool that comes to mind is a meeting. Meetings are probably the most misused organizational tools in existence. Some people have never participated in an effective meeting in their entire careers. It's no wonder, then, that pointless, ineffective meetings perpetuate themselves year after year, like an organizational disease. If meetings are so often ineffective, why even bother with them? There are some very good reasons:

- Face-to-face communication builds trust and buy-in.
- E-mails, memos, reports, and communication often are misinterpreted; a meeting allows issues to be clarified in real time.
- Complex decision making often requires the dynamic interaction of a meeting.
- Sensitive topics are best handled in the discreet setting of a meeting, rather than in a manner that can be misused.

Clearly, meetings can be an important communication tool. The challenge is to make them effective and a good value for the resources consumed. Meetings, like any other system or tool, require procedural guidelines to be effective. Approaching meetings in an ad hoc manner will guarantee poor results. Meetings must be carefully planned and controlled. Keep in mind that effective meetings:

■ *Have a clear purpose.* This seems obvious, but many meetings are held "because it seemed like a good idea," not because there was any compelling purpose. The purpose of the meeting must be clear to everyone involved. In fact, the meeting's purpose should be one of the first points addressed. Having a clearly understood purpose helps the meeting stay on track and prevents it from going in too many different directions

■ *Have a facilitator.* This person helps keep the meeting moving in the right direction. He or she manages the personalities and ensures that conflicts are resolved constructively. He or she makes sure that the meeting actually produces something. The facilitator's role can be carried out by the person who called the meeting or by someone who has no stake whatsoever in the outcome. Someone must act as a facilitator, however. In very sophisticated work teams, the meeting attendees can act as co-facilitators.

■ *Have firm start and stop times.* Meetings consume valuable time, not only of those in attendance but also of people who otherwise would have been working with meeting attendees. It's critical, then, to use the time in the most efficient manner possible. One way is to start the meeting on time. Don't keep a meeting from starting because one or two people haven't arrived. Start the meeting at the time it's supposed to start. Once people understand that the meeting really will start on time, they'll make whatever plans are necessary to be there on time.

The end time is just as important. When that time arrives, draw the discussions to a close. Provide a quick recap of the decision and/or actions that were agreed upon during the meeting and adjourn. If the agenda wasn't completely addressed, schedule a later meeting to discuss the remaining items. Few situations are as frustrating as a meeting that runs past its end time.

■ *Produce decisions and/or actions.* I've walked out of countless meetings, only to ask myself, "What exactly was decided in there?" When it's not clear to everyone what decisions and/or actions result from a meeting, then it was a waste of time. Even information sharing meetings produce decisions and/or actions. Consider the following decision from a meeting to communicate a six-month strategic plan: "We confirmed that all participants understood our strategic plan for the next six months and how their functions will contribute." Here's an action that might result from the very same meeting: "All managers agreed to communicate the revised objectives to their subordinates within three business days." The bottom line: *All* meetings produce actions and/or decisions. Prior to adjourning a meeting, it's very helpful to recap the actions and decisions that have resulted so there's no confusion or ambiguity.

■ *Are recorded.* People have short memories. No matter how adamantly participants agreed to actions and decisions, within a week many will have forgotten what was decided. Record the output of meetings. This can be done simply, efficiently, and unceremoniously. Just get the details of the meeting recorded in the body of a memo or an e-mail. Some people refer to these as meeting minutes. The quicker that meeting minutes or their equivalent are generated after the meeting, the better. Make sure they're distributed to all participants as well as important stakeholders who weren't present. Remember that almost nobody reads business communications longer than two pages, so strive to limit the minutes to the fewest words possible that still communicate the needed information.

■ *Include participants who are prepared.* Part of the reason that meetings continue for long past the promised end time is that the participants aren't prepared. Background information must be explained, data must be interpreted, every angle must be discussed to exhaustion, and opinions must be formulated. Much of this could take place outside the meeting, in the days or weeks preceding it. Strive to provide meeting participants with as much preliminary information as possible, so that when the meeting actually starts everyone will be that much closer to producing actions and decisions. An agenda published in advance is another way to prepare participants for their roles. It also helps the meeting to stay on track and on purpose.

Meetings can be one of the most powerful communication tools in existence. With some basic planning and management, organizations can get the full benefit from their meetings and minimize the disruption that so many associate with these forums.

ORDERLINESS

An organization's orderliness reflects the mindset of the people working there. Cluttered and disorganized organizations reflect a chaotic way of doing business, and chaos breeds errors and defects. Clean and orderly organizations reflect a systematic way of doing business, which leads to consistency, efficiency, and the prevention of problems. It's a simple equation.

Orderliness is a term used to encompass a number of basic concepts:

■ Housekeeping
■ Personal pride in work areas

■ Junk removal
■ Identifying supplies and materials
■ Instructions for critical tasks
■ Timely information
■ An overall drive toward simplicity

The tenets of orderliness defined above represent common sense. Unfortunately, many people are too busy to trouble themselves with common sense. Despite the fact that a lack of orderliness causes personnel to work harder; some people refuse to embrace orderliness as a principle of success, arguing that it's nothing more than an attempt to dictate behaviors that naturally differ from person to person. Personal preference or not, some degree of orderliness is critical to success. What sorts of problems occur in the absence of orderliness?

■ *Customers are disgusted.* Attentive customers are quick to note poor housekeeping and disorganization. In fact, for many businesses, housekeeping is a make-or-break issue for retaining customers and gaining new ones. Orderliness has a conscious and subconscious effect on customers' psyches. There's no way to calculate the effect disorderliness has on customer perceptions and satisfaction.

■ *Processes are delayed.* Disorganization inevitably results in misplaced tools, equipment, products, and supplies. Things just seem to disappear when orderliness erodes. Missing resources inevitably cause delays.

■ *Employees are demoralized.* Disorganization and chaos prevent employees from performing at their best, and they begin to feel powerless. No matter how hard they try, errors still occur. A demoralized workforce can in itself be a terminal cancer for the organization.

■ *Products are defective.* How can a quality product possibly be produced in an organization that's chaotic and disorganized? Only through pure chance. When root cause analysis is performed on defective products, it often reveals one of these culprits: inaccurate information (e.g., instructions or specifications), unavailable supplies or materials, misidentified products, or an environment that doesn't encourage best efforts. All of these can be overcome through an orderly and systematic approach to managing.

Disorderliness clearly erodes competitiveness, customer satisfaction, and overall success. What, then, are some indicators of an organization that practices orderliness? The answers are quite simple:

- Desks cleared of piles of paper, mail, and clutter
- Materials remaining on desks clearly organized
- Floors free of obstructions and dirt
- Grounds and work areas free of litter
- Bathrooms clean and hygienic
- Parking areas free of debris and garbage
- Simple and graphic procedures
- Visible proof that personnel use procedures
- Graphic signs used to communicate important messages
- Information available where it's needed
- Designated locations for tools and equipment
- Tools and equipment actually stored in their assigned locations
- Prominent visual designations for walkways, storage locations, forklift alleys, and nonconforming-material segregation areas
- Obsolete tools, equipment, and supplies removed (sold, bartered, given away, recycled, or scrapped)
- Obsolete finished goods removed (sold, bartered, given away, recycled, or scrapped)
- Storage containers clearly labeled
- Individual products, materials, and supplies identified
- Smallest possible production lots in use
- Production driven by actual demand
- Employees who are cross-trained and able to move quickly from one task to another
- Equipment that's flexible and able to accommodate changes easily
- Shared responsibility for housekeeping
- Preoccupation with safety and removal of safety hazards
- Managers who not only preach orderliness but also practice it

For organizations interested in embracing orderliness as an operating principle, a checklist has been included in this chapter's appendix, on page 146. The orderliness and safety checklists work well as a one-two punch for getting facilities cleaned up, organized, and safe.

These basic disciplines of orderliness are also reflected in the Japanese manufacturing concept of 5S. These each represent similar tasks. Whether the initiative is called 5S, orderliness, or something else really doesn't matter. The disciplines comprise a basic foundation for success. Like all disciplines, common sense must be applied. Orderliness can be applied in an excessive manner, bordering on obsession. The following absurdities are commonly found during 5S implementations:

■ Labeling common objects such as coffeemakers, common office machines, and staplers. What value do these labels add? If someone doesn't know what a stapler is, then they probably won't be able to read the label. Don't go overboard labeling things. Identify objects in cases where the identification will eliminate confusion and errors.

■ Completely removing all personal photographs, keepsakes, certificates, and decorations from work areas. Although these objects might not play a critical role in accomplishing the job at hand, they're important from a psychological standpoint. Apply some common sense. Personal items shouldn't be allowed to clutter and distract, but they shouldn't be banned outright, either.

■ Excessive motivational signs telling people what they already know: "Waste is Your Enemy," "Everybody Succeeds With Teamwork," "Only *You* Can Do It Right The First Time." These messages are condescending to the few people who notice them, and invisible to everybody else. Replace unnecessary posters with specific information about safety hazards, progress toward objectives, team successes, and other things that people really need to know about. Use good sense with all signs. Even smart signs can distract, and distractions cause problems.

Apply the concepts of orderliness in a wise, even-handed manner, and your organization will experience fewer delays, errors, customer complaints, and accidents.

RECOGNITION

All humans crave recognition. It's a universal need. Whether you're a manager in Atlanta or a mechanic in Ankara, you want to be recognized for your efforts. Simply put, getting recognized feels good. The employee certainly benefits from recognition, but the organization benefits as well. How do employees and the organization specifically benefit from recognition? Let's take an inventory:

■ Employees receive unequivocal feedback on their performance.

■ Employees understand that their efforts make a difference.

■ Employees' pride and self-esteem are reinforced.

■ Other personnel understand that the organization values its people and cares about their success.

■ Employees feel more loyal to the organization and its objectives. They begin to feel that they are the organization, as opposed to simply an employee.

■ Employees are more willing to go above and beyond in a way that money can't buy.

■ The organization increases its advantage over competitors.

Recognition is, by its very nature, an extrinsic reward system. There is no way that extrinsic rewards can replace intrinsic rewards in an organization that is building a culture of continual improvement. Intrinsic rewards include such things as a sense of accomplishment and importance, challenging work, task variety, skill development, and personal growth. Intrinsic rewards must be cultivated first, then extrinsic rewards (such as a recognition system) can be developed. A recognition system supplements intrinsic rewards, but is no substitute for them. Recognition is presented as the final topic in this chapter because it is one of the final processes that should be implemented, and only after intrinsic rewards and motivation have emerged as part of the organization's culture.

Clearly, it makes good business sense to recognize employees. However, recognition is a complicated issue. With the best of intentions, organizations often implement recognition systems that backfire and create exactly the opposite effects than were intended. Embracing the following principles will ensure that recognition achieves the desired results.

Recognition should be:

■ *Public.* Recognition must be made in front of the larger organization. This might constitute a process, division, facility, or the entire corporation. The nature of the recognition will obviously influence the context within which it's given, but it's important to do so in front of a group. The public nature of the recognition reinforces its significance for both the recipient and the rest of the organization. Public recognition also means that it's made in person as opposed to by telephone, e-mail, fax, or some other remote means.

■ *Available to everyone.* For it to have a positive effect on organizational culture, recognition must be available to anyone. Many companies offer forms of recognition, but often they're available only to certain employees, such as production or hourly personnel. The rationale apparently is that recognition is only important to people in certain parts of the organization. This is absurd, of course; recognition is important to everyone. Make sure your organization's recognition system rewards the efforts of all personnel.

■ *Dignified.* Recognition must create a feeling of dignity in the person who receives it. This can be achieved by building a ceremony, such as a company meeting or holiday dinner, around the recognition. Dignity is also enhanced by a degree of seriousness and formality in the proceedings. This doesn't mean everyone must be stiff, humorless, and dressed in uncomfortable clothes; it simply means that the presentation possesses a degree of seriousness that lets all personnel know how much special contributions are valued.

■ *Symbolic.* Recognition must have symbolic value, something that's lasting and that serves as a continual reminder of the performance being recognized. Keepsakes such as letters, certificates, plaques, trophies, and paperweights are very effective in adding symbolism to the recognition process. Symbolic keepsakes inspire motivation and pride long after the date and time of recognition have passed.

■ *Nonmonetary.* Are people motivated by money? Of course. That's why they work. But exceptional performances often are motivated by something more complex and mysterious. Offering money as part of your recognition system is a bad idea. It cheapens the recognition by attempting to affix a monetary value. Not every effort, contribution, idea, or suggestion can be monetarily quantified with any degree of accuracy. Instead, the organization should provide honest, symbolic recognition. Issues of fairness also arise when money enters into the recognition process. The only time money is an effective part of the formula is when it's purely symbolic. Some organizations provide a crisp, new dollar bill whenever someone is recognized. Employees even get their CEO to sign the dollars, and the currency often gets framed and displayed on the wall. In this way, the monetary reward has the power as a certificate.

Sustained, outstanding performance should be matched with increased compensation and promotions, of course. If the organization has the resources to increase the pay of its star performers, then it's wise to do so. This is different from the type of recognition I'm describing, however. Keep your day-to-day recognition system free of monetary awards, and you'll have far fewer headaches.

■ *Presented by top management.* Recognition is more significant when it's delivered by top management. The message is that top management is aware of everyone's performance and contributions and is thankful for the effect outstanding efforts have on the organization's success. In reality, especially in larger organizations, top managers are somewhat removed from individual performances. When executive leadership is involved in recognizing someone, it heightens the event's significance and symbolism and also helps to humanize top management. It shows that the executives are down in the trenches recognizing the people who do the organization's heavy lifting.

■ *Prompted by a variety of actions.* The use of objective, data-oriented criteria is often the best way to make decisions. However, not everyone's performance can be characterized in this way. Superior performances take many forms. Make sure your recognition system can capture the full range of actions and performances deserving of notice. Don't restrict its scope by declaring, "Here are the three things that will trigger recognition." Inevitably, a policy of this sort will prevent you from recognizing someone who really deserves it, simply because their performance doesn't meet the predetermined criteria. Give your system plenty of flexibility and discretion.

■ *Not tied to a rigid time frame.* You've seen the "Employee of the Month" and "Employee of the Quarter" awards many times. The only problem with establishing a time frame of this sort is that the recognition becomes predictable and routine. There might not even be any especially outstanding performance during the month, but it's that time again… heck, just pick someone! Forced decisions like this degrade the recognition system. In truth, an organization might go months without identifying performance worthy of special recognition, only to erupt in a blaze of outstanding performances within the same week. Recognize personnel when their performance dictates it, not when the calendar does.

Now that we've determined *how* people should be recognized, we must determine *who* will be recognized. What process can be employed for identifying personnel worthy of special recognition? Many organizations convene a management committee comprised of a cross section of the organization for this purpose. I generally oppose decision making by committee, but it's effective for this purpose. A reasonably small committee of managers—no more than ten people—meets regularly to discuss the special achievements of personnel in their areas and agree on persons deserving of recognition.

Even better than letting a management committee decide who deserves recognition is to let personnel themselves decide. People who are answering phones, packaging products, troubleshooting equipment, and servicing customers see very quickly which performances are worthy of recognition. An easy way to capture the perspectives of personnel is through a card system of some sort. Organizations put catchy titles on the cards, such as "We're writing you up... for being excellent!" and provide adequate space for all the relevant details. Blank cards can be distributed to various areas or made available electronically. Anybody at any level is authorized to complete a card, detailing the person to be recognized and what he or she did to deserve it. Completed cards are publicly displayed on a wall or bulletin board, and all the persons who were "written up" receive formal recognition according to the guidelines above. Using the entire workforce to identify outstanding performances offers a number of advantages:

■ It quickly builds an environment that's supportive and team-oriented.
■ It's a more accurate way of identifying outstanding contributions because the people submitting names have firsthand knowledge of the performances.
■ It generally results in more evenly distributed recognition and avoids the trap of recognizing only those who work within the most visible functions.
■ It helps people to feel involved and express their opinions.
■ It shatters the notion that the recognition system is just a tool for management to play favorites by recognizing those who rigidly conform.

The public display of completed cards serves as a constant reminder of not only the personnel recognized but also the inclusive nature of the recognition system. The message is, "We support one another in our jobs and take the time to provide recognition where it's deserved." Few systems are as powerful as an effective recognition system. The effect on organizational culture is significant and immediate. An example of a recognition submission card is shown in Figure 8.2.

Figure 8.2: Sample Recognition Card

(Front of Card)

We're Writing You Up... For Being Excellent!

Please be on the lookout for outstanding performances on the part of your peers, subordinates, and supervisors. When you locate actions worthy of recognition, please complete the spaces below and submit the completed card to the "We're Writing You Up!" box in the main office area.

Date: ___/___/___ Your name: _____

Your department: _____ Your phone number: (   ) _____

Name of person to be recognized: _____

What did this person do? _____

_____

_____

(Back of Card)

Review and Recognition

Reviewed by: _____ Date: ___/___/___

Recognition given: _____

_____

_____

_____

_____

_____

_____

_____

DOS AND DON'TS OF BUILDING THE CULTURE

Building a culture of continual improvement is an investment that takes place over an extended period of time. Heed the following dos and don'ts as your organization embarks on its journey of cultural evolution:

✔ *Do seek out and eliminate safety hazards.* Few issues contribute to an environment of respect and continual improvement as much as safety does.

✔ *Do remove status differentiators.* These tell everyone that some people are better than others, which is counterproductive to everyone working together to drive continual improvement.

✔ *Do provide teams with direction and facilitation.* Whether they've been formed to attack a problem or propose an improvement, teams need clear direction and skilled facilitation.

✔ *Do recognize employees in a simple, public, and dignified manner.* Recognition is one of the most powerful tools available for building a culture that mobilizes all personnel to make improvements.

✔ *Do plan meetings.* The planning that goes into meetings shouldn't be elaborate, but it's critical if the meeting is to produce something of value. Basic planning elements include a clear purpose for the meeting, firm start and stop times, prepared participants, and a designated person to record the meeting and the output of decisions and/or actions.

✔ *Do clean up and organize.* It's impossible for personnel to perform at their best in an environment where clutter, disarray, and poor housekeeping reign.

✘ *Don't expect an organization's culture to change overnight.* Cultures are formed over many years and after implementing countless actions and decisions. Do the right things, and gradually the organization's culture will start moving toward one that facilitates improvement.

✘ *Don't start a suggestion system unless you're willing to make it a success.* They require a significant amount of time and energy to manage. Starting a suggestion system, only to let it die a few months later, does nothing to instill a culture of improvement.

✘ *Don't use cash or prizes as part of your recognition system.* Instead of motivating people, these rewards will only cause mistrust and rancor when people perceive inequalities in the rewards' distribution.

✘ *Don't get too fancy with company newsletters.* They're meant to communicate important information in a timely fashion, not to impress the readers. Keep it simple and easy to produce.

✘ *Don't go overboard with orderliness.* Getting cleaned up and organized is important, but use common sense and don't become obsessive about it.

Chapter Eight Appendix

Figure 8.3: Safety Checklist

Completed by: _____ Date: ___/___/___ Time: _____

Area(s) inspected: _____

Does the organization periodically identify hazards in the workplace, assess their risks, and apply appropriate controls?

❏ Yes ❏ No ❏ N/A

Comments: _____

_____

Are all new and revised procedures evaluated for safety issues?

❏ Yes ❏ No ❏ N/A

Comments: _____

_____

Is the work area clean and organized?

❏ Yes ❏ No ❏ N/A

Comments: _____

_____

Are all spills of liquid and debris cleaned up promptly?

❏ Yes ❏ No ❏ N/A

Comments: _____

_____

Is lighting adequate for work to be carried out in a safe manner?

❏ Yes ❏ No ❏ N/A

Comments: _____

_____

Are all building exits marked and unobstructed?

❏ Yes ❏ No ❏ N/A

Comments: _____

_____

Are all doors that are neither exits nor leading to exits marked to prevent confusion in an emergency?

❏ Yes ❏ No ❏ N/A

Comments: _____

_____

Is there an emergency response plan in place? If yes, are personnel trained in the plan?

❑ Yes   ❑ No   ❑ N/A

Comments: _____

_____

Does the facility perform periodic emergency response drills?

❑ Yes   ❑ No   ❑ N/A

Comments: _____

_____

Are evacuation maps posted and maintained current?

❑ Yes   ❑ No   ❑ N/A

Comments: _____

_____

Are emergency phone numbers posted and maintained current?

❑ Yes   ❑ No   ❑ N/A

Comments: _____

_____

In areas where forklifts or other vehicles operate, are walking pathways clearly marked?

❑ Yes   ❑ No   ❑ N/A

Comments: _____

_____

Do forklifts and/or other vehicles sound their horns when passing through pedestrian areas or when approaching intersections?

❑ Yes   ❑ No   ❑ N/A

Comments: _____

_____

Are all accidents and near misses submitted to formal corrective or preventive action?

❑ Yes   ❑ No   ❑ N/A

Comments: _____

_____

Do all machines and equipment have appropriate guards in place to prevent injury?

❑ Yes   ❑ No   ❑ N/A

Comments: _____

_____

Are all chemicals identified correctly and stored in an appropriate manner?

❑ Yes   ❑ No   ❑ N/A

Comments: _____
_____

Are material safety data sheets available to employees?

❑ Yes   ❑ No   ❑ N/A

Comments: _____
_____

Do floors, pathways, and ladder rungs have appropriate antislip protection to prevent falls?

❑ Yes   ❑ No   ❑ N/A

Comments: _____
_____

Do all employees receive safety training prior to performing job duties?

❑ Yes   ❑ No   ❑ N/A

Comments: _____
_____

Do contractors receive orientation on safety rules and guidelines prior to beginning work?

❑ Yes   ❑ No   ❑ N/A

Comments: _____
_____

Is all personal protection equipment (e.g., gloves, hard hats, hearing protection, goggles, etc.) maintained in good working order?

❑ Yes   ❑ No   ❑ N/A

Comments: _____
_____

Do personnel use personal protective equipment in the correct manner?

❑ Yes   ❑ No   ❑ N/A

Comments: _____
_____

Are fire extinguishers available throughout the work area? If yes, are they periodically inspected?

❑ Yes   ❑ No   ❑ N/A

Comments: _____
_____

Do all stairways, fixed ladders, and catwalks have handrails and appropriate safety guards?

❑ Yes   ❑ No   ❑ N/A

Comments: _____

_____

Are all combustible materials and debris stored in an appropriate manner?

❏ Yes   ❏ No   ❏ N/A

Comments: _____

_____

Reviewed by: _____ Date: ___/___/___

Actions to be taken:

_____

_____

Corrective/preventive action No., if applicable:

_____

_____

Figure 8.4: Sample Newsletter

The Weekly Buzz
May 15, 2003

Thanks to everyone who was instrumental in getting that big order for Blowhard Corp. out the door this week. The lead time was nearly impossible, but we did it. Great work! I've already heard back from the people in Blowhard's production department, and they said the parts have worked perfectly. This is just one more example of everyone working hard to get the job done. Please remember that we'll celebrate this success during the communication meeting next week.

While I was traveling last week, I was able to take a look at the parts that were rejected by Behemoth Inc. The defects appear to have been caused by us. I've instructed Behemoth to return the entire shipment, at a total cost that will likely exceed $17,000. Please pay special attention to all solders and connections! We can't survive with this type of return. After our QA people have had a chance to take a look at the returns, we'll incorporate a review of them into our next companywide communication meeting.

Please join me in congratulating the team in shipping for their idea of changing the loading pattern of component boxes within the larger corrugated boxes. This will save the company more than $40,000 per year in reduced packaging materials. Thanks to Jim, Davy, Joyce, Roxie, and Bill for this terrific idea.

As usual, I'm highlighting one of our key measures in the newsletter. This week the spotlight is on percentage of perfect orders. Please let your supervisor know if you need clarification on how you contribute to this metric. Remember that next month's internal audit will focus on everyone's understanding of key measures and how they're improved.

Keep up the good work,
Peter Buzz
President and CEO

Figure 8.5: Orderliness Checklist

Completed by: _____ Date: ___/___/___ Time: _____

Area(s) inspected: _____

Are desks free of piles of paper, mail, and clutter?

❑ Yes ❑ No ❑ N/A

Comments: _____
_____

Are floors and walkways clean and free of obstructions?

❑ Yes ❑ No ❑ N/A

Comments: _____
_____

Are the grounds around the facility free of litter, cigarette butts, and other debris?

❑ Yes ❑ No ❑ N/A

Comments: _____
_____

Are bathrooms clean and hygienic?

❑ Yes ❑ No ❑ N/A

Comments: _____
_____

Do procedures include graphics and the simplest possible text?

❑ Yes ❑ No ❑ N/A

Comments: _____
_____

Do personnel use the procedures?

❑ Yes ❑ No ❑ N/A

Comments: _____
_____

Are important messages communicated using graphic signs and posters?

❑ Yes ❑ No ❑ N/A

Comments: _____
_____

Is information (e.g., specifications, instructions, processes data, etc.) available at the point of use?

❑ Yes ❑ No ❑ N/A

Comments: _____

Do all tools and equipment have an assigned location?

❏ Yes   ❏ No   ❏ N/A

Comments: _____

_____

Are tools and equipment kept in their assigned locations when they are not being used?

❏ Yes   ❏ No   ❏ N/A

Comments: _____

_____

Are all walkways, vehicle paths, and storage areas clearly marked?

❏ Yes   ❏ No   ❏ N/A

Comments: _____

_____

Have obsolete product, materials, supplies, and equipment been removed?

❏ Yes   ❏ No   ❏ N/A

Comments: _____

_____

Are all storage containers labeled (unless it's obvious what is stored in the container)?

❏ Yes   ❏ No   ❏ N/A

Comments: _____

_____

Are all products, materials, and supplies identified (unless it's obvious what the products, materials, and supplies are)?

❏ Yes   ❏ No   ❏ N/A

Comments: _____

_____

Is production driven by actual demand?

❏ Yes   ❏ No   ❏ N/A

Comments: _____

_____

Can employees easily move from one activity to another, based on the demands of the organization?

❏ Yes   ❏ No   ❏ N/A

Comments: _____

_____

_____

Can equipment accommodate fast and frequent changes?
❑ Yes   ❑ No   ❑ N/A
Comments: _____   _____   _____
Is everyone in the organization involved in housekeeping?
❑ Yes   ❑ No   ❑ N/A
Comments: _____   _____   _____
Is there evidence that top management has personally adopted a philosophy of orderliness for their own activities?
❑ Yes   ❑ No   ❑ N/A
Comments: _____   _____   _____
Reviewed by: _____ Date: ___/___/___
Actions to be taken: _____   _____
Corrective/preventive action No., if applicable: _____   _____

SUGGESTION SYSTEM PROCEDURE

1. Purpose/scope

This procedure's overall objective is to provide a systematic method for all personnel to propose their ideas and suggestions. It's not intended that this system replace other means for communicating suggestions; it simply provides a convenient method for employees to channel improvement ideas to decision makers.

The guidelines set forth in this document cover all company locations. Any questions should be directed to the quality manager.

2. Procedure

2.1. Employees are encouraged to complete a Process Improvement Recommendation (PIR) card when they want to communicate ideas, improvements, problems, or potential problems with their process to management.

2.2. Completed PIR cards are routed to the employee's supervisor.

2.3. The supervisor will review the PIR submission and sign the bottom of the card if the PIR is appropriate for evaluation. PIR submissions that deal with gripes, rumors, accusations, company policy, or personnel issues are not appropriate for evaluation.

2.4. Approved PIR cards are forwarded to the PIR administrator, who assigns a tracking number. Each PIR card is assigned to an individual for investigation and action as appropriate.

2.5. The person assigned to the PIR will record on the back of the card what action was taken.

2.6. Within an appropriate period of time, the employee who submitted the PIR is made aware of the action taken in regard to their PIR. The employee will initial and date the PIR card in the space labeled response date to show that they've received a response.

2.7. The process manager will verify that action taken in regard to the PIR has been effective. If effective, the manager will date the bottom of the card in the space labeled "completion date."

2.8. The PIR administrator will ensure that PIRs are adequately addressed and that employees receive a response in a timely fashion.

Chapter Nine

Conclusion

In This Chapter
- Involve Top Management
- Appoint a Champion
- Communicate Vigorously
- Cultivate the Culture

The individual steps of the continual improvement process interact and complement one another like gears in a machine. They depend on each other to drive the organization forward. Is it possible to get positive results from isolated steps in the process? Yes, but the results won't be optimal by any means. It's nearly impossible to separate the steps without compromising the process's ability to produce results.

Develop a plan for implementing each of the components of the continual improvement process. Implement them methodically and at your own pace, but implement all of them. With an integrated continual improvement process, your organization will have an insurance policy against uncertainty. The organization will control its own fate because it will always be making improvements—maybe not huge improvements, but definitely continual improvement. Every day, in every process, some seemingly small aspect of the enterprise will be improving. Over time, the cumulative effect of this will be astounding.

Four essential threads are woven in the fabric of the continual improvement process. Keep these in mind as you implement your improvement strategy:

■ *Involve top management.* The continual improvement process stands no chance of success if top management isn't 100-percent sold on its benefits.

That's one of the reasons that the process starts with determining mission, strategy, and key measures. Besides being a logical starting point, those are subjects that top managers are universally interested in. Grab top management's attention and keep them involved daily.

■ *Appoint a champion.* All successful efforts have a champion. To rally the organization and keep everyone focused, you'll need a charismatic leader, someone to champion the continual improvement process, facilitate its tools, and tout its successes. The champion also acts as the liaison to top management. In the most progressive organizations, top management is the continual improvement champion. This is the ideal state, but exceptional results can be achieved with a wide range of other personnel filling the champion role.

■ *Communicate vigorously.* The lubricating oil that flows through the gears of the continual improvement process is communication. None of the processes described in this book will function without communication. In fact, many of the processes are, at their cores, communication processes. This entire book could be summarized in the statement, "Communicate vigorously, analyze the message and its implications, and take appropriate action." The importance of communication can't be overstated.

■ *Cultivate the culture.* Most of the processes described here are concrete and analytical. However, organizational culture is different. It's amorphous, fluid, and difficult to grasp. For this reason, many people simply overlook culture as a variable of the continual improvement process. This is a huge mistake. Culture will ultimately determine whether continual improvement becomes a core organizational process, or just a flash-in-the-pan program that fades away after a few months.

Now the time has come to convert theory to reality. Get out there and start building your continual improvement process. It could make the difference between life and death for your organization. With a little energy, discipline, and desire, the continual improvement process can become an unstoppable machine for your long-term success.

Bibliography

Brigham, Eugene F., and Louis C. Gapenski. *Financial Management: Theory and Practice* (Seventh Edition). Fort Worth: The Dryden Press, 1994.

Crosby, Philip B. *Quality Is Free: The Art of Making Quality Certain.* New York: McGraw-Hill, Inc., 1979.

Deming, W. Edwards. *Out of the Crisis.* Cambridge: Massachusetts Institute of Technology, Center for Advanced Engineering Study, 1986.

———. *The New Economics for Industry, Government, Education.* Cambridge: Massachusetts Institute of Technology, Center for Advanced Engineering Study, 1993.

Feigenbaum, Armand G. *Total Quality Control* (Third Edition). New York: McGraw-Hill, Inc., 1983.

Hill, Charles W., and Gareth R. Jones. *Strategic Management: An Integrated Approach* (Third Edition). Boston: Houghton Mifflin Company, 1995.

Imai, Masaaki. *Kaizen: The Key to Japan's Competitive Success.* New York: McGraw-Hill, Inc., 1986.

Juran, J. M., and Frank M. Gryna. *Quality Planning and Analysis.* New York: McGraw-Hill Inc., 1980.

Kaplan, Robert S., and David P. Norton. *The Balanced Scorecard.* Boston: Harvard Business School Press, 1996.

Whetten, David A., and Kim S. Cameron. *Developing Management Skills* (Third Edition). New York: HarperCollins College Publishers, 1995.

Index